CONTENTS

ReadING People Deeper	1
Why Reading People Matters	3
Chapter 1: The Importance of Context	6
Chapter 2: Baseline Observation	10
Chapter 3: Verbal and Paraverbal Cues	15
Chapter 4: Facial Expressions - The Windows to the Soul	21
Chapter 5: The Eyes - A Powerful Source of Information	28
Chapter 6: The Mouth - More Than Just Words	34
Chapter 7: Body Gestures - Speaking Without Words	39
Chapter 8: Posture - Projecting Confidence and Authority	46
Chapter 9: Breathing - The Rhythm of Emotions	53
Chapter 10: The Chest and Shoulders - Power and Vulnerability	60
Chapter 11: Appearance and Clothing - The Silent Messages We Send	64
Chapter 12: Proxemics - The Language of Space	71
Chapter 13: Detecting Deception - Unmasking the Lies	77
Chapter 14: Personality Types - Understanding Underlying Motivations	85
Chapter 15: Motives and Behavior - Deciphering the "Why"	92
Chapter 16: Seduction and Attraction - The Nonverbal Dance	99

Chapter 17: Influencing Others - The Power of Nonverbal Persuasion — 107

Chapter 18: Mastering Your Own Nonverbal Communication — 115

CONCLUSION — 124

READING PEOPLE DEEPER

Unmasking the True Thoughts and Feelings of Others by Decoding Body Language

Sarah Thompson

No part of this book may be reproduced or transmitted in any form whatsoever, electronic, or mechanical, including photocopying, recording, or by any informational storage or retrieval system without express permission from the author.

Copyright © 2024 JNR Publishing
All rights reserved

WHY READING PEOPLE MATTERS

In our daily interactions, whether personal or professional, we constantly communicate through more than just our words. Our facial expressions, gestures, posture, and tone of voice all convey a wealth of information about our thoughts, feelings, and intentions. The ability to accurately interpret these nonverbal cues is a powerful skill that can lead to greater understanding, empathy, and success in all areas of life.

By learning to read people more effectively, we gain valuable insights into their true motivations and emotions, even when their words may not align with their body language. This allows us to navigate social situations more adeptly, build stronger relationships, and communicate with greater clarity and impact.

In professional settings, reading nonverbal cues can give us an edge in negotiations, interviews, and leadership roles. We can detect when someone is holding back information, feeling uncertain, or not fully engaged, and adjust our approach accordingly. In personal relationships, being attuned to nonverbal communication helps us be more responsive to our loved ones' needs, avoid misunderstandings, and deepen our emotional connections.

Additionally, enhancing our skills in perceiving people can safeguard us from being deceived or manipulated. By recognizing the telltale signs of dishonesty or ill intent, we can make more informed decisions and safeguard our own interests. In an age where "fake news" and social media deception are rampant, the ability to discern genuine from insincere communication is more crucial than ever.

The Limitations of "Natural" Reading

While some people seem to have a natural gift for reading others, relying solely on intuition or "gut feelings" can be misleading. Our own biases, past experiences, and emotions can cloud our judgment and cause us to project our own thoughts and feelings onto others. This tendency, known as solipsism, can lead to misinterpretations and faulty conclusions.

To become a skilled reader of people, we need to balance empathy with objective, analytical observation. Empathy allows us to put ourselves in someone else's shoes and understand their perspective, but it can also make us more susceptible to being influenced by their emotions or manipulated by their words. Analytical observation, on the other hand, involves stepping back and assessing nonverbal cues objectively, without letting our own feelings interfere.

By combining empathy and analysis, we can gain a more accurate and complete picture of what someone is really thinking and feeling. We can validate our intuitive hunches with concrete evidence, and avoid jumping to conclusions based on limited or ambiguous information.

Throughout this book, we will explore the key principles and techniques for mastering the art of reading people. We will delve into the intricacies of nonverbal communication, from the subtlest facial expressions to the most overt gestures and postures. We will learn how to establish baselines, recognize patterns, and interpret clusters of signals in context. And we will discover how to apply these skills in real-world situations, from detecting deception to building rapport and influencing others.

Whether you are a business leader, salesperson, teacher, therapist, or simply someone who wants to improve your relationships and social interactions, this book will provide you with a comprehensive guide to decoding the silent language of the body. By the end, you will have a newfound appreciation for the power of nonverbal communication, and the tools to read people with greater accuracy, empathy, and insight. Let the journey begin.

PART 1: FOUNDATIONS OF NONVERBAL COMMUNICATION

CHAPTER 1: THE IMPORTANCE OF CONTEXT

One of the most crucial principles in reading nonverbal cues is understanding the context in which they occur. A gesture or expression can have vastly different meanings depending on the situation, the relationship between the people involved, and the cultural norms at play. Without considering these contextual factors, we risk misinterpreting signals and drawing inaccurate conclusions.

Universal vs. Culturally Specific Cues

Some nonverbal cues are considered universal, meaning they are expressed and understood similarly across cultures. These include basic emotional expressions like happiness, sadness, anger, fear, surprise, and disgust. When we see someone smiling with crinkled eyes, for example, we intuitively know they are experiencing genuine joy or amusement, regardless of their cultural background.

However, many other nonverbal signals vary significantly across cultures. In some Middle Eastern countries, for instance, standing close to someone and maintaining strong eye contact are signs of respect and engagement, whereas in Western cultures, the same behaviors might be perceived as aggressive or inappropriate. Similarly, hand gestures like the "thumbs up" or "OK" sign have positive connotations in some countries, but are considered offensive in others.

To accurately read nonverbal cues, we must be aware of these cultural differences and adapt our interpretations accordingly. This requires not only learning about specific customs and norms, but also being open-minded, observant, and willing to adjust our assumptions based on the context.

Situational Factors Influencing Nonverbal Behavior

Even within the same culture, nonverbal behavior can vary greatly depending on the specific situation and the roles and relationships of the people involved. In a job interview, for example, the interviewee may display more nervous, submissive body language, such as fidgeting, avoiding eye contact, or speaking in a lower tone of voice. The interviewer, on the other hand, may project confidence and authority through an upright posture, direct eye contact, and expansive gestures.

Similarly, in a romantic setting, nonverbal cues like prolonged eye contact, mirroring of postures, and gentle touching can signal attraction and intimacy. In a confrontational situation, however, the same individuals may exhibit aggressive or defensive body language, such as invading personal space, clenching fists, or crossing arms tightly.

Other situational factors that can influence nonverbal behavior include:

• The physical environment: People tend to be more relaxed and open in comfortable, familiar settings, and more guarded or anxious in unfamiliar or threatening ones.

• The emotional state of the individuals: Strong emotions like stress, fear, or excitement can override normal nonverbal patterns and lead to exaggerated or incongruent expressions.

• The power dynamics: Those in positions of authority or higher status often display more dominant, expansive nonverbals, while those in subordinate roles may show more submissive, constrictive cues.

By taking these situational factors into account, we can better understand the underlying drivers of someone's nonverbal behavior and interpret their cues more accurately.

Reading Clusters of Signals, Not Isolated Gestures

Another key principle in effective people-reading is to look for clusters of nonverbal cues, rather than focusing on isolated gestures or expressions. Relying too heavily on a single signal can lead to misinterpretation, as the same behavior can have different meanings in different contexts or for different individuals.

For example, crossed arms are often associated with defensiveness, resistance, or closing oneself off. However, someone may also cross their arms simply because they are cold, or because it is a comfortable resting position for them. To determine the true meaning of this cue, we need to look for other signals that can provide additional context and clarity.

If the crossed arms are accompanied by a furrowed brow, tense facial muscles, and leaning away from the other person, it is more likely to indicate genuine discomfort or disagreement. On the other hand, if the individual is still smiling, nodding along, and maintaining an open stance otherwise, the crossed arms may be a less significant or meaningful gesture.

By observing multiple nonverbal channels simultaneously - facial expressions, eye movements, posture, gestures, voice tone, etc. - we can paint a more complete and reliable picture of someone's inner state and intentions. The more congruent and consistent the cluster of cues, the more confident we can be in our interpretation.

Importantly, we must also consider the individual's baseline behavior and look for deviations or changes over time, as discussed in the next chapter. What may be a meaningful signal for one person could be a normal, habitual gesture for another. Only by establishing a reference point and tracking patterns over time can we make accurate judgments about the significance of someone's nonverbal behavior.

In summary, context is king when it comes to reading people effectively. By being attuned to cultural differences, situational factors, and the interplay of multiple nonverbal signals, we can avoid common pitfalls and gain deeper, more nuanced insights into the thoughts, feelings, and motivations of those around us. Mastering this contextual awareness is the foundation upon which all other people-reading skills are built.

CHAPTER 2: BASELINE OBSERVATION

In order to accurately interpret someone's nonverbal cues, it is essential to first establish their baseline behavior - that is, their typical or "normal" patterns of expression and body language. Only by understanding what is usual for an individual can we identify meaningful deviations or changes that may signify a shift in their thoughts, emotions, or intentions.

Establishing Normal Behavior Patterns for Individuals

Everyone has their own unique way of communicating nonverbally, influenced by factors such as their personality, cultural background, life experiences, and social roles. Some people may naturally be more expressive and animated, using expansive gestures and facial expressions to convey their ideas and feelings. Others may be more reserved or stoic, maintaining a relatively flat affect and minimal body movement.

To establish a baseline for an individual, observe them over time and across different situations. Pay attention to their:

• Facial expressions: What is their resting face like? Do they tend to smile, frown, or maintain a neutral expression? How quickly and intensely do their expressions change?

• Eye contact: Do they make direct, sustained eye contact, or do they tend to look away or down? How do their eyes move when they are thinking, listening, or speaking?

• Posture: Do they typically sit or stand in an upright, slouched, or relaxed position? How do they hold their head, shoulders, and limbs?

• Gestures: Are their hand and arm movements fluid and expansive, or constrained and close to the body? Do they use a lot of illustrative gestures when speaking?

• Voice: What is their typical speaking pace, volume, pitch, and tone? Do they often pause, stutter, or use filler words?

By observing these and other nonverbal patterns over time, you can create a mental "profile" of the individual's baseline behavior. This will serve as a reference point against which you can compare their cues in specific situations and interactions.

It's worth noting that baselines can shift depending on the situation and the individual's emotional state. For example, someone who is normally calm and composed may become more fidgety and agitated when under stress or pressure. Similarly, a person who is usually reserved may become more animated and expressive when discussing a topic they are passionate about.

To account for these variations, try to observe the individual in as many different contexts as possible - at work, at home, in social settings, etc. Look for patterns that remain consistent across situations, as well as those that change depending on the environment or the task at hand. The more comprehensive your understanding of their baseline behavior, the more accurately you can interpret deviations from it.

Identifying Deviations from the Baseline as Potential Indicators

Once you have a solid grasp of someone's normal nonverbal patterns, you can start to look for deviations or changes that may indicate a shift in their thoughts, feelings, or intentions. These deviations can be subtle or overt, and can occur in any nonverbal channel - facial expressions, eye movements, posture, gestures, voice, etc.

For example, let's say you have a colleague who typically maintains an upright, confident posture during meetings, with open body language and direct eye contact. One day, you notice that they are slouching in their chair, avoiding eye contact, and crossing their arms tightly. This marked change from their usual behavior may suggest that they are feeling defensive, insecure, or disengaged from the discussion.

Similarly, if a friend who is normally animated and expressive suddenly becomes still and withdrawn, it may indicate that something is bothering them or they are holding back their true feelings. Or if a usually calm and measured speaker starts to fidget, stumble over their words, or speak more rapidly, it may be a sign of nervousness, uncertainty, or deception.

The key is to look for deviations that are significant and sustained, rather than fleeting or minor. A single instance of a changed behavior may not be meaningful on its own, but a pattern of deviations over time or across different situations can provide valuable insights into the person's inner state and motivations.

The direction and intensity of the deviation need to be considered. Is the person displaying more or less of a certain behavior than usual? Is the change subtle or extreme? A slight increase in fidgeting, for example, may indicate mild nervousness or discomfort, while a dramatic increase may suggest high levels of anxiety or stress.

By comparing someone's current nonverbal cues to their established baseline, you can make more accurate judgments about the meaning and significance of their behavior. This allows you to respond more appropriately and empathetically to their needs and concerns, and to navigate interactions with greater skill and sensitivity.

Recognizing Conscious vs. Unconscious Nonverbal Signals

Another important distinction to make when reading people is between conscious and unconscious nonverbal signals. Conscious cues are those that an individual deliberately chooses to display, often to convey a specific message or impression. Unconscious cues, on the other hand, are those that occur automatically and without intention, often revealing the person's true thoughts and feelings.

For example, someone may consciously smile and maintain eye contact to appear friendly and engaged, even if they are actually feeling bored or annoyed. This type of "social smile" is a learned behavior that is used to smooth interactions and maintain positive relationships. While it may be a genuine expression of goodwill in some cases, it can also be used to mask negative emotions or manipulate others' perceptions.

In contrast, unconscious nonverbal cues are more difficult to control and often provide a more reliable window into someone's inner state. These may include:

• Microexpressions: Fleeting facial expressions that last a fraction of a second and reveal true emotions before the individual has a chance to suppress or mask them. • Pupil dilation: An automatic response of the eyes that can indicate interest, attraction, or arousal. • Blushing or blanching: Involuntary changes in skin color that can signify embarrassment, shame, or fear. • Pacifying behaviors: Self-soothing gestures like touching the face, hair, or neck, which can indicate stress, anxiety or discomfort. • Leakage: Nonverbal cues that "leak out" despite an individual's efforts to conceal them, such as a brief smirk or eye roll.

By learning to recognize and differentiate between conscious and unconscious nonverbal signals, you can gain a more accurate and nuanced understanding of someone's true thoughts and intentions. While conscious cues can provide useful information about how a person wants to be perceived, unconscious cues often reveal more authentic and unfiltered insights.

It's important to keep in mind that even unconscious cues can be confusing or misleading at times. Some people may have learned to suppress or control their automatic responses through practice or training, while others may have idiosyncratic or culturally specific expressions that differ from the norm. As with all aspects of people-reading, it's essential to consider the full context and look for clusters of cues rather than relying on any single signal alone.

The objective of baseline observation is to acquire a comprehensive, personalized understanding of the nonverbal patterns and tendencies of every individual. By paying close attention to their typical behaviors and identifying meaningful deviations from the norm, you can gain valuable insights into their thoughts, feelings, and motivations - even when their words may not match their actions. This skill is the foundation of effective people-reading, and one that can be continually refined and expanded through practice and experience.

CHAPTER 3: VERBAL AND PARAVERBAL CUES

While nonverbal cues are often the most revealing and reliable indicators of someone's true thoughts and feelings, verbal and paraverbal cues - the words people use and how they say them - can also provide valuable insights into their inner world. By paying close attention to the content, structure, and delivery of someone's speech, we can gain a more complete and nuanced understanding of their emotions, attitudes, and intentions.

Voice: Volume, Speed, Pitch, Tone, and Their Emotional Implications

The way someone speaks - their vocal characteristics and patterns - can convey a wealth of information about their emotional state and personality. Some key aspects of Voice to consider include:

- **Volume**: Loudness or softness of speech can indicate confidence, assertiveness, or emotional intensity. Speaking too quietly may suggest shyness, insecurity, or a lack of conviction, while speaking too loudly can come across as aggressive, domineering, or overcompensating.
- **Speed**: The pace at which someone speaks can reflect their level of excitement, anxiety, or thoughtfulness. Rapid speech may indicate enthusiasm, nervousness, or a desire to control the conversation, while slower speech can convey calmness,

deliberation, or hesitation.

- **Pitch**: The highness or lowness of someone's voice can communicate their emotional state and level of arousal. A higher pitch may suggest excitement, surprise, or stress, while a lower pitch can indicate relaxation, sadness, or seriousness.
- **Tone**: The overall quality and inflection of someone's voice can reveal their underlying attitudes and feelings. A warm, friendly tone conveys openness and positivity, while a cold, sarcastic tone suggests displeasure or hostility. Upward inflections at the end of sentences may indicate uncertainty or seeking approval, while downward inflections convey confidence and assertiveness.

By tuning into these vocal cues and patterns, we can gain deeper insight into someone's emotional landscape and interpersonal style. For example, a person who consistently speaks in a soft, hesitant voice with frequent upward inflections may be signaling insecurity, anxiety, or a need for validation. On the other hand, someone who speaks in a loud, rapid, and emphatic manner may be conveying excitement, urgency, or a desire to dominate the conversation.

It's important to note, however, that vocal cues can vary widely across individuals and cultures, and should always be interpreted in context. Some people may naturally have a higher or lower pitched voice, faster or slower speech, or a more monotone delivery, without necessarily implying any particular emotional state. As with all aspects of people-reading, it's essential to establish a baseline for each individual and look for deviations or inconsistencies that may be telling.

Word Choice: Analyzing Language for Subtle Hints and Inconsistencies

In addition to how someone speaks, the specific words and phrases they use can also provide clues to their thoughts, feelings, and motivations. By paying close attention to someone's language patterns and choices, we can identify subtle hints, inconsistencies, or hidden meanings that may not be immediately apparent.

Some key aspects of language to consider include:

- *Pronouns*: The use of "I," "we," "you," or "they" can indicate a person's level of ownership, involvement, or distance from a topic or situation. For example, someone who frequently uses "we" statements may be signaling a sense of teamwork, shared responsibility, or a desire to affiliate with others. In contrast, someone who relies heavily on "you" or "they" statements may be deflecting accountability or creating psychological distance.
- *Qualifiers*: Words like "maybe," "sometimes," "kind of," or "a little" can suggest uncertainty, ambivalence, or a lack of commitment to a statement or idea. Overuse of qualifiers may indicate that someone is hedging, avoiding directness, or lacking confidence in their own assertions.
- *Intensifiers*: Words like "very," "extremely," "absolutely," or "literally" can add emphasis or conviction to a statement, but can also be used to overcompensate for insecurity or deception. When someone frequently uses intensifiers, especially in situations where they are not warranted, it may suggest that they are trying too hard to convince others (or themselves) of something.
- *Euphemisms and minimizers*: Using mild, indirect, or vague language to describe negative or sensitive topics can be a way of avoiding discomfort, responsibility, or confrontation. For example, someone who refers to a serious mistake as a "little mishap" or a major conflict as a "slight disagreement" may be downplaying the severity of the situation or their own role in it.
- *Inconsistencies and contradictions*: When someone's words do not match their actions, or when they make statements that are logically inconsistent or contradictory, it can be a red flag

for deception, confusion, or lack of integrity. For instance, if a colleague claims to have "always been a team player," but consistently takes credit for others' work or refuses to collaborate, their words and behaviors are not aligning.

By carefully analyzing someone's language patterns and choices, we can gain valuable insights into their thought processes, emotional states, and underlying motives. However, it's crucial to remember that language is complex and context-dependent, and that individual words or phrases can have different meanings or connotations for different people and situations.

As with all aspects of people-reading, the key is to look for patterns and inconsistencies over time, rather than jumping to conclusions based on a single instance or statement. By combining an awareness of language cues with an understanding of nonverbal signals and contextual factors, we can paint a more complete and accurate picture of someone's inner world and intentions.

Silence and Pauses: Understanding the Meaning of Unspoken Communication

Just as the words we speak can convey important information about our thoughts and feelings, the words we *don't* speak - the silences, pauses, and hesitations in our communication - can also be rich with meaning and insight. In many cases, what someone chooses *not* to say can be just as revealing as what they do say, if not more so.

Some common types of silence and their potential meanings include:

- **Thoughtful silence**: When someone pauses before responding to a question or statement, it may indicate that they are carefully considering their words, weighing multiple perspectives, or trying to formulate a diplomatic response. This type of silence suggests engagement,

deliberation, and a desire to communicate effectively.
- **Uncomfortable silence**: Long, awkward pauses or sudden drops in conversation can signal tension, disagreement, or unspoken issues between individuals. If someone usually quick to respond or fill conversational gaps suddenly goes silent, it may indicate that they are holding back, feeling defensive, or uncertain how to proceed.
- **Evasive silence**: When someone repeatedly dodges questions, changes the subject, or gives brief, non-committal responses, it may suggest that they are hiding something, avoiding responsibility, or reluctant to engage on a particular topic. Evasive silence can be a red flag for deception or lack of transparency.
- **Shocked or surprised silence**: A sudden intake of breath, widening of the eyes, or slackening of the jaw, followed by a momentary silence, can indicate that someone has been caught off guard, stunned, or taken aback by new information. This type of silence may precede a strong emotional response or a need to regroup and process.
- **Contemplative or meditative silence**: In some contexts, extended periods of silence can be a sign of deep reflection, introspection, or mindfulness. When someone is grappling with complex emotions, engaging in creative work, or practicing meditation or prayer, they may naturally fall into a state of focused, intentional silence.

The meaning of silence and pauses can vary widely depending on the person, culture, and situation, just like all nonverbal cues. In some contexts, such as negotiations or interviews, strategic silence can be used as a power play or a way to unsettle the other party. In other cases, such as in some Asian cultures, extended pauses in conversation are a sign of respect and thoughtfulness, rather than discomfort or avoidance.

To accurately interpret the meaning of silence in any given interaction, it's essential to consider the full range of verbal, nonverbal, and contextual cues available. By paying attention to subtle shifts in body language, facial expressions, and vocal tone, as well as the content and flow of the conversation, we can gain a more nuanced understanding of what someone's silence may be communicating.

PART 2: DECODING THE BODY - A HEAD-TO-TOE GUIDE

CHAPTER 4: FACIAL EXPRESSIONS - THE WINDOWS TO THE SOUL

The face is often considered the most expressive and revealing part of the body, capable of conveying a wide range of emotions, attitudes, and intentions through a complex interplay of muscle movements and micro-expressions. By learning to read and interpret facial cues accurately, we can gain valuable insights into someone's inner world and emotional state, even when their words may not match their true feelings.

Microexpressions: Decoding Fleeting Expressions for Hidden Emotions

One of the most powerful tools in the face reader's toolkit is the ability to spot and decipher microexpressions - brief, involuntary facial expressions that flash across the face in a fraction of a second, revealing a person's true emotions before they have a chance to control or mask them. These fleeting expressions are believed to be universal across cultures, and can provide a window into someone's authentic feelings, even when they are trying to conceal them.

The seven basic emotions that are most commonly associated with microexpressions are:

1. Happiness
2. Sadness
3. Anger
4. Fear
5. Surprise
6. Disgust
7. Contempt

Each of these emotions is characterized by a specific set of facial muscle movements, such as the upward pull of the lips in a genuine smile, the raising of the inner eyebrows in sadness, or the wrinkling of the nose in disgust. By learning to recognize these subtle, fleeting expressions, we can gain a more accurate picture of someone's true feelings, even when their words or overt behaviors may be sending a different message.

For example, imagine you are in a meeting with a colleague who is presenting a new idea to the team. On the surface, they appear confident and enthusiastic, speaking with conviction and using expansive gestures. However, at one point in the presentation, you catch a brief flash of fear or uncertainty cross their face - a slight widening of the eyes, a quick downturn of the mouth, or a tensing of the forehead. This microexpression, though only lasting a fraction of a second, suggests that beneath their confident exterior, your colleague may be feeling anxious or unsure about their idea, and may benefit from additional support or reassurance.

Effectively detecting microexpressions requires practicing observing facial movements in slow motion, which can be done by watching videos of social interactions or by studying photographs of different emotional expressions. Over time, you can train your eye to catch these subtle, fleeting cues in real-time conversations and use them to gain a deeper understanding of the person's true feelings and needs.

Eye Movements: Direction, Duration, and Their

Connection to Thoughts and Memories

In addition to facial expressions, eye movements can also provide valuable clues about someone's internal thought processes, memories, and emotions. By observing the direction, duration, and quality of someone's gaze, we can gain insight into what they may be thinking or feeling, even if they are not explicitly verbalizing it.

Some common eye movement patterns and their potential meanings include:

- *Upward gaze*: When someone looks up and to the left, it may indicate that they are accessing visual memories, trying to remember something they have seen before. When they look up and to the right, it may suggest that they are engaging in visual construction, imagining or creating a mental image of something new.
- *Lateral gaze*: Looking to the left can indicate that someone is recalling auditory memories, such as remembering a conversation or a piece of music. Looking to the right may suggest auditory construction, such as imagining how a new song or sound might go.
- *Downward gaze*: When someone looks down and to the left, it may indicate that they are accessing feelings or kinesthetic sensations, such as remembering a physical experience or emotion. Looking down and to the right may suggest internal dialogue or self-talk.
- *Darting eyes*: Rapid, unfocused eye movements can be a sign of anxiety, nervousness, or discomfort. If someone is constantly scanning the room or avoiding eye contact, it may suggest that they are feeling insecure, overwhelmed, or evasive.
- *Prolonged stare*: Maintaining eye contact for an extended period can be a sign of interest, attraction, or dominance, depending on the context and the individual. However, an unwavering, unblinking stare can also be interpreted as

threatening or intimidating.

It's important to note that eye movement patterns are not always reliable indicators of specific thoughts or emotions, and can vary widely across individuals and cultures. Some people may have idiosyncratic or habitual eye movements that do not necessarily correspond to the general patterns described above. Additionally, certain neurological conditions or visual impairments can affect eye movements in ways that are not related to internal mental states.

Accurately interpreting eye cues is a key aspect of nonverbal communication, as it is important to consider them in context and in conjunction with other facial, bodily, and verbal signals. By paying attention to patterns and inconsistencies in someone's gaze, and by comparing them to their baseline behavior and the situation at hand, we can gain valuable insights into their thoughts, feelings, and intentions.

Smiles: Differentiating Between Genuine and Fake Smiles

The smile is one of the most universally recognized and powerful facial expressions, capable of conveying a wide range of positive emotions, from happiness and amusement to warmth and affection. However, not all smiles are created equal - some are genuine reflections of inner joy and connection, while others may be polite, forced, or even deceptive. Learning to differentiate between authentic and fake smiles is a critical skill for anyone seeking to read people accurately and build trusting, authentic relationships.

The key to distinguishing between genuine and fake smiles lies in understanding the specific facial muscles involved in each type of expression. A genuine, heartfelt smile - also known as a Duchenne smile - involves the activation of both the zygomatic major muscle, which pulls the corners of the mouth upward, and the orbicularis oculi muscle, which crinkles the skin around the eyes and creates "crow's feet" wrinkles. This combination of muscle movements creates a full, warm, and natural-looking expression that is difficult to fake.

In contrast, a polite or social smile - also known as a non-Duchenne smile - involves only the zygomatic major muscle, without the activation of the orbicularis oculi. This type of smile may appear more stiff, forced, or asymmetrical, and may not reach the eyes in the same way as a genuine smile. People may use polite smiles to conform to social norms, to mask negative emotions, or to appear agreeable or cooperative, even when they are not feeling genuinely happy or connected.

Some common signs of a fake or polite smile include:
- Lack of eye involvement (no crinkling around the eyes)
- Asymmetry (one side of the mouth raised higher than the other)
- Abrupt onset or offset (the smile appears or disappears too quickly)
- Incongruence with other facial or bodily cues (e.g., smiling while frowning or tensing the jaw)

To spot the difference between genuine and fake smiles, it's important to pay close attention to the entire face, not just the mouth. Look for the telltale signs of orbicularis oculi activation, such as raised cheeks, narrowed eyes, and wrinkles around the outer corners of the eyes. Notice the timing and duration of the smile, and whether it seems to flow naturally from the person's overall demeanor and conversation.

It's also important to consider the context and the relationship between the individuals involved. In some cases, a polite or social smile may be entirely appropriate and expected, such as when greeting a stranger or participating in a formal event. In other cases, a lack of genuine smiling may indicate discomfort, disconnection, or hidden negative emotions that need to be addressed.

By learning to read smiles accurately and empathetically, we can gain valuable insights into someone's true feelings and intentions, and respond in ways that build trust, rapport, and authentic connection. Whether in personal relationships or professional interactions, the ability to differentiate between genuine and fake smiles is a powerful tool for navigating complex social dynamics and creating more meaningful, fulfilling interactions.

Common Smile Types: Tight-Lipped, Twisted, Drop-Jaw, Sideways-Looking-Up

In addition to distinguishing between genuine and fake smiles, it's also useful to be aware of some common types of smiles and their potential meanings. While not exhaustive, the following categories can provide a helpful framework for interpreting different smile expressions and the emotions or intentions they may convey.

1. **Tight-Lipped Smile**: This type of smile involves pressing the lips together tightly, without showing the teeth. It can indicate a range of emotions, from mild discomfort or uncertainty to outright disapproval or disdain. A tight-lipped smile may suggest that the person is holding back their true feelings, is reluctant to engage, or is trying to maintain a polite or neutral demeanor despite internal tension or disagreement.
2. **Twisted Smile**: A twisted smile is characterized by a sideways pulling of one corner of the mouth, often accompanied by a slight narrowing or rolling of the eyes. This expression can convey sarcasm, irony, or a sense of wry amusement, as if the person is privy to a private joke or is gently mocking the situation at hand. Twisted smiles can also indicate mixed feelings or a sense of superiority or condescension.
3. **Drop-Jaw Smile**: Also known as a "gaping grin," this type of smile involves a wide, open-mouthed expression,

often accompanied by raised eyebrows and a slight backward tilt of the head. A drop-jaw smile can indicate genuine excitement, surprise, or delight, as if the person is so overwhelmed with positive emotion that they can't contain their response. However, in some cases, a drop-jaw smile can also be a sign of feigned or exaggerated enthusiasm, especially if it appears abrupt or out of sync with the rest of the person's demeanor.
4. **Sideways-Looking-Up Smile**: This coy or playful smile involves a slight tilt of the head, a raising of one corner of the mouth, and a sidelong glance upward, often through partially lowered eyelashes. The sideways-looking-up smile can indicate flirtation, coyness, or a sense of shared mischief or conspiracy, as if the person is inviting you to join them in a private moment of amusement or connection. However, this smile can also be used manipulatively, as a way of disarming or charming others for ulterior motives.

When interpreting these or any other types of smiles, it's crucial to consider the full context of the interaction, including the person's baseline behavior, their relationship to you and others present, and the broader social and cultural norms at play. A tight-lipped smile from a normally expressive friend, for example, may carry a very different meaning than the same smile from a professional colleague in a formal business setting.

By familiarizing yourself with these and other common smile types, and by practicing observing and decoding facial expressions in various contexts, you can develop a more nuanced and accurate understanding of the emotional landscapes and interpersonal dynamics at work in your daily interactions. Whether you're aiming to build stronger personal relationships, navigate complex professional environments, or simply gain deeper insight into the people around you, the ability to read and respond to different types of smiles is a valuable skill to cultivate.

CHAPTER 5: THE EYES - A POWERFUL SOURCE OF INFORMATION

The eyes are often considered the most expressive and revealing part of the face, capable of conveying a wide range of emotions, intentions, and unspoken messages. By learning to read and interpret eye cues accurately, we can gain valuable insights into someone's inner world, even when their words or overt behaviors may be sending a different message.

Eye Contact: Duration, Avoidance, and Its Connection to Confidence, Trust, and Deception

One of the most basic and powerful forms of eye communication is eye contact - the act of looking directly into someone's eyes during an interaction. The duration, frequency, and quality of eye contact can provide important clues about a person's emotional state, level of engagement, and degree of honesty or deception.

In general, maintaining appropriate eye contact is seen as a sign of confidence, trustworthiness, and social skill. People who are comfortable making and sustaining eye contact are often perceived as more likable, competent, and persuasive than those who avoid or break eye contact frequently. In many cultures, direct eye contact is also a way of showing respect, attention, and interest in the other person.

The interpretation of eye contact can change based on the situation and people involved. In some situations, prolonged or intense eye contact may be interpreted as a sign of aggression, dominance, or sexual interest, rather than mere friendliness or attention. In other cases, breaking eye contact or looking away briefly can signal thoughtfulness, self-reflection, or a need for privacy, rather than discomfort or evasion.

When it comes to detecting deception, the role of eye contact is complex and often misunderstood. Contrary to popular belief, liars do not necessarily avoid eye contact more than truth-tellers. In fact, some studies have shown that liars may actually maintain more deliberate and prolonged eye contact than usual, in an attempt to appear honest and convincing.

Instead of focusing solely on the amount of eye contact, it's important to look for other cues that may indicate discomfort, anxiety, or inconsistency, such as:

- Blinking more rapidly or slowly than usual
- Shifting the eyes from side to side or up and down
- Touching or rubbing the eyes or surrounding areas
- Squinting or widening the eyes excessively
- Failing to match eye contact with other facial expressions or body language

By paying attention to these and other subtle eye cues, and by considering them in the context of the overall interaction and relationship, we can gain a more accurate and nuanced understanding of someone's true feelings, intentions, and level of truthfulness.

Pupil Dilation: An Involuntary Signal of Interest, Attraction, or Fear

Another important aspect of eye communication is pupil dilation - the involuntary expansion or contraction of the black center of the eye in response to various stimuli. While pupil size is primarily regulated by the amount of light entering the eye, it can also be influenced by emotional and cognitive factors, such as interest, attraction, or fear.

In general, when we are excited, curious, or attracted to something or someone, our pupils tend to dilate, allowing more light to enter the eye and enhancing our visual perception. This response is thought to be an evolutionary adaptation that helps us gather more information about potentially important or rewarding stimuli.

Conversely, when we are feeling scared, threatened, or averse to something, our pupils may constrict, reducing the amount of light entering the eye and signaling a defensive or avoidant response. This narrowing of the pupils is often accompanied by other signs of fear or disgust, such as widening of the eyes, flaring of the nostrils, or pulling back of the head.

Research has shown that pupil dilation can be a reliable indicator of sexual or romantic interest, with both men and women showing larger pupil sizes when viewing attractive faces or erotic images. In fact, some studies suggest that people unconsciously mimic the pupil sizes of those they are attracted to, as a way of signaling mutual interest and creating a sense of rapport.

However, it's important to note that pupil dilation is not always a definitive sign of attraction or positive regard. In some cases, dilated pupils may simply indicate a state of general arousal or intensity, regardless of the specific emotion being experienced. Moreover, certain drugs, medical conditions, and lighting conditions can also affect pupil size, making it important to consider the full context when interpreting this cue.

To accurately read pupil dilation, it's best to establish a baseline for the individual and the environment, and to look for noticeable changes in pupil size that coincide with specific emotional or cognitive responses. By combining this information with other facial and bodily cues, we can gain a more complete and reliable picture of someone's inner state and motivations.

Squinting: Indicating Skepticism, Dislike, or Uncertainty

Squinting is another common eye behavior that can provide valuable insights into someone's thoughts and feelings. This facial expression involves a slight narrowing or tightening of the eyes, often accompanied by a furrowing of the brow or a pursing of the lips.

In general, squinting can indicate a range of negative or skeptical emotions, such as:

- **Suspicion or doubt**: When someone is unsure about the truth or validity of what they are hearing or seeing, they may squint as a way of "looking closer" or scrutinizing the information more carefully.
- **Dislike or disapproval**: Squinting can also be a sign of aversion or negative judgment, as if the person is literally trying to "block out" or minimize something they find unpleasant or objectionable.
- **Confusion or uncertainty**: In some cases, squinting may simply indicate a state of cognitive strain or effort, as the person tries to make sense of complex or ambiguous information.
- **Physical discomfort**: Squinting can also be a reflexive response to bright lights, glare, or other visual stressors, or to physical sensations like pain or fatigue.

When interpreting squinting, it's important to consider the timing, duration, and intensity of the expression, as well as any accompanying verbal or nonverbal cues. A brief, mild squint during a conversation may simply indicate thoughtfulness or concentration, while a prolonged, pronounced squint accompanied by other signs of discomfort or disagreement may signal a more serious issue that needs to be addressed.

In some cases, chronic squinting or a habit of "squinching" the eyes may be a learned behavior or a sign of an underlying vision problem, rather than a genuine emotional response. By comparing someone's squinting behavior to their baseline and to the context of the interaction, we can gain a more accurate sense of its meaning and significance.

Sideway Glances: Revealing Uncertainty, Nervousness, or Withholding Information

Sideway glances, also known as "shifty eyes" or "darting glances," can be another informative eye cue in interpersonal communication. This behavior involves a quick, furtive movement of the eyes to the side, often accompanied by a turning of the head or a shifting of the body posture.

In general, sideway glances can indicate a range of emotions or intentions, such as:

- **Nervousness or anxiety**: When someone is feeling uncomfortable, insecure, or "on the spot," they may glance to the side as a way of avoiding direct eye contact or seeking an escape route.
- **Deception or withholding**: In some cases, sideway glances may be a sign that someone is being evasive, dishonest, or withholding important information. This cue is often accompanied by other signs of discomfort or inconsistency, such as fidgeting, stammering, or contradicting oneself.
- **Distraction or divided attention**: Sideway glances can also simply indicate that someone is momentarily distracted by something in their environment, or that they are trying to multitask or process multiple streams of information at once.
- **Flirting or social signaling**: In some contexts, a quick, playful sideway glance can be a way of flirting, building rapport, or signaling a shared understanding or inside joke with another person.

As with other eye cues, it's crucial to interpret sideway glances in the context of the overall interaction and relationship, and to look for patterns or clusters of behavior that may provide a more reliable indication of someone's true thoughts and feelings. A single, fleeting glance to the side may not mean much on its own, but a repeated pattern of sideway glances accompanied by other signs of discomfort, evasion, or inconsistency may warrant further attention or follow-up.

By learning to recognize and decode these and other subtle eye cues, we can gain a deeper, more nuanced understanding of the people around us, and respond in ways that build trust, rapport, and authentic connection. Whether in personal relationships or professional interactions, the eyes truly are the windows to the soul - and a powerful source of insight for those who know how to read them.

CHAPTER 6: THE MOUTH - MORE THAN JUST WORDS

While the eyes may be the windows to the soul, the mouth is often considered the gateway to the mind - a powerful source of both verbal and nonverbal communication that can reveal a wealth of information about someone's thoughts, feelings, and intentions. From the words we speak to the subtle movements of the lips, jaw, and tongue, the mouth is a highly expressive and dynamic part of the face that can provide valuable insights into a person's inner world.

Lip Compression: A Sign of Stress, Discomfort, or Withholding Information

One of the most common and telling mouth cues is lip compression - the act of pressing the lips together tightly, often accompanied by a subtle pursing or thinning of the mouth. This behavior can indicate a range of negative emotions or mental states, such as:

- **Stress or anxiety**: When we are feeling overwhelmed, nervous, or under pressure, we may unconsciously compress our lips as a way of "holding in" or controlling our emotions. This cue is often accompanied by other signs of tension, such as jaw clenching, neck tightness, or shallow breathing.
- **Disagreement or disapproval**: Lip compression can also be a sign of withheld opinion or unspoken objection,

as if the person is literally "biting their tongue" to avoid saying something negative or confrontational. This cue may be especially noticeable in situations where the person feels obligated to remain polite or diplomatic, despite their true feelings.

- **Concentration or determination**: In some cases, lip compression may simply indicate a state of intense focus, effort, or self-control, as the person tries to "power through" a difficult task or challenge. This type of lip compression is often more brief and task-specific than the stress- or disapproval-related varieties.
- **Deception or withholding**: Lip compression can also be a sign that someone is being evasive, dishonest, or withholding important information. When combined with other cues of discomfort or inconsistency, such as averted eye contact, fidgeting, or vocal strain, lip compression may suggest that the person is not being fully truthful or forthcoming.

When interpreting lip compression, it's important to consider the timing, duration, and intensity of the behavior, as well as any accompanying facial expressions or body language. A brief, mild lip press during a conversation may simply indicate thoughtfulness or hesitation, while a prolonged, pronounced compression accompanied by other signs of stress or discomfort may signal a more serious issue that needs to be addressed.

By learning to recognize and respond to lip compression and other mouth cues, we can gain a deeper understanding of the unspoken messages and emotional undercurrents in our interactions, and communicate with greater empathy, clarity, and effectiveness.

Lip Purse: Indicating Disagreement, Consideration, or Searching for Alternatives

Another common and expressive mouth behavior is the lip purse - a subtle puckering or rounding of the lips, often accompanied by a slight outward protrusion or "pouty" appearance. This cue can convey a range of emotions or mental states, depending on the context and the individual:

- **Disagreement or skepticism**: In some cases, a lip purse may indicate that the person is feeling doubtful, unconvinced, or mildly disapproving of what they are hearing or seeing. This cue is often accompanied by a slight tilting of the head, a furrowing of the brow, or a narrowing of the eyes, as if the person is "scrutinizing" or "questioning" the information being presented.
- **Consideration or contemplation**: A lip purse can also signal that the person is deep in thought, pondering a decision, or weighing different options or perspectives. In this context, the lip purse may be accompanied by a far-off gaze, a slight nodding of the head, or a gentle stroking of the chin or cheek, as the person "mulls over" the situation at hand.
- **Flirting or playfulness**: In more lighthearted or playful interactions, a lip purse may be used as a flirtatious or teasing gesture, often accompanied by a coy smile, a batting of the eyelashes, or a tilting of the head. This type of lip purse is usually more exaggerated and intentional than the contemplative or skeptical varieties, and may be used to signal romantic interest or to build rapport and connection.
- **Self-soothing or self-control**: In some cases, a lip purse may simply be a self-soothing or self-regulating behavior, as the person tries to calm or center themselves in a stressful or uncertain situation. This type of lip purse is often more subtle and unconscious than the other varieties, and may be accompanied by other self-touch behaviors, such as rubbing the forehead or touching the neck.

Interpreting lip purses in context and observing clusters or patterns of behavior can better reveal the person's true thoughts and feelings when compared to other mouth cues. A single, fleeting lip purse may not carry much meaning on its own, but a repeated pattern of lip pursing accompanied by other signs of disagreement, contemplation, or self-soothing may warrant further attention or follow-up.

By attuning ourselves to these subtle yet expressive mouth behaviors, we can gain valuable insights into the unspoken dynamics of our interactions, and respond with greater tact, empathy, and skill.

Tongue Displays: Licking Lips, Tongue Jutting, and Their Connection to Stress, Deception, or Playfulness

In addition to the lips and jaw, the tongue can also provide important clues about a person's emotional state, level of comfort, and potential for deception or manipulation. Some common tongue behaviors and their possible meanings include:

- **Lip licking**: Licking the lips is a common self-soothing or moisturizing behavior that can indicate nervousness, tension, or concentration. When someone is feeling stressed, anxious, or "put on the spot," they may unconsciously lick their lips as a way of relieving dryness or calming themselves down. However, excessive or deliberate lip licking can also be a sign of deception or manipulation, as the person tries to appear more relaxed or confident than they actually feel.
- **Tongue jutting**: Tongue jutting involves a quick, forward thrust of the tongue between the lips, often accompanied by a slight widening of the eyes or a tilting of the head. This behavior can indicate a range of emotions or intentions, depending on the context. In children or playful adults, tongue jutting may be a sign of lighthearted teasing, silliness, or mischief. In more serious or competitive situations, tongue jutting can signal a sense of victory, self-satisfaction, or "getting away with something," as if the person is savoring a private triumph or secret.
- **Tongue biting or chewing**: Biting or chewing on the tongue, often unconsciously, can be a sign of intense concentration, nervousness, or self-restraint. When someone is struggling

to focus on a difficult task, to hold back a strong emotion, or to avoid saying something inappropriate, they may bite down on their tongue as a way of redirecting their energy or maintaining self-control. In some cases, visible tongue biting or chewing may also indicate lying or withholding, as the person tries to suppress or regulate their verbal responses.

- **Tongue protrusion**: A slight, often unconscious protrusion of the tongue between the lips can be a sign of focused attention, absorption, or "flow" in an activity. This behavior is often seen in young children as they work on a drawing or puzzle, but can also occur in adults engaged in creative or mentally engaging tasks. In social situations, a subtle tongue protrusion may indicate interest, curiosity, or a desire to "taste" or explore a new idea or experience.

Interpreting tongue behaviors in context and identifying patterns or clusters of cues can provide a more reliable indication of the person's true thoughts and feelings, just like with other nonverbal cues. By paying attention to these subtle, often unconscious tongue displays, we can gain a deeper understanding of the emotional and psychological dynamics at play in our interactions, and respond with greater insight, empathy, and skill.

CHAPTER 7: BODY GESTURES - SPEAKING WITHOUT WORDS

Beyond the face, the body is a rich source of nonverbal communication, capable of conveying a wide range of emotions, attitudes, and intentions through gestures, postures, and movements. By learning to read and interpret body language accurately, we can gain valuable insights into a person's inner world, even when their words or facial expressions may be ambiguous or misleading.

Hand Gestures: Open Palms, Pointing, Interlocked Fingers, and Their Cultural Variations

One of the most expressive and dynamic aspects of body language is hand gestures - the various ways we use our hands and fingers to emphasize, illustrate, or punctuate our verbal messages. Some common hand gestures and their possible meanings include:

- **Open palms**: Showing the palms of the hands is often seen as a sign of openness, honesty, and transparency. When someone holds their hands out with the palms facing up, they may be indicating a willingness to share, receive, or collaborate. In some contexts, open palms can also be a sign of surrender, vulnerability, or a lack of aggression, as if the person is saying "I have nothing to hide."
- **Pointing**: Pointing with the index finger is a common way of directing attention, emphasizing a point, or singling out a

specific person or object. However, the meaning of pointing can vary widely across cultures and contexts. In some societies, pointing is considered rude or aggressive, while in others it is a normal part of animated conversation. Pointing can also be used to assign blame, express accusation, or establish dominance, depending on the situation and the individuals involved.

- **Interlocked fingers**: Clasping the hands together with interlocked fingers is often seen as a sign of anxiety, tension, or self-restraint. When someone is feeling nervous, uncertain, or "on the spot," they may unconsciously interlock their fingers as a way of self-soothing or regaining control. In some cases, interlocked fingers may also indicate a closed or guarded attitude, as if the person is "holding back" or "keeping something in."
- **Steepling**: Steepling involves touching the tips of the fingers together, often with the palms separated and the fingers pointing upward. This gesture is often seen as a sign of confidence, authority, or intellectual precision, as if the person is "making a point" or "getting to the heart of the matter." However, excessive or prolonged steepling can also come across as arrogant, domineering, or self-important, especially if accompanied by other signs of superiority or condescension.

The meaning of hand gestures can vary widely across cultures, and what is deemed normal or polite in one society may be seen as offensive or inappropriate in another. For example, the "thumbs up" gesture is a common sign of approval or agreement in many Western countries, but in some Middle Eastern cultures it is considered a vulgar or insulting gesture.

Similarly, the "OK" sign made by touching the thumb and index finger together is a positive signal in the United States, but in Brazil it is an offensive gesture with sexual connotations.

To accurately interpret hand gestures, it's essential to consider the cultural context, the relationship between the individuals involved, and any accompanying verbal or nonverbal cues that may provide additional meaning or nuance. By attuning ourselves to these subtle yet powerful forms of nonverbal communication, we can navigate cross-cultural interactions with greater understanding, respect, and effectiveness.

Arm Crossing: A Defensive Posture, Signaling Discomfort or Disagreement

Another common and often misunderstood body gesture is arm crossing - the act of folding the arms across the chest, often with the hands tucked under the biceps or gripping the upper arms. While this posture is often associated with defensiveness, resistance, or closed-mindedness, its meaning can vary depending on the context and the individual.

Some possible interpretations of arm crossing include:

- **Discomfort or insecurity**: When someone feels uncomfortable, anxious, or exposed, they may cross their arms as a way of creating a physical barrier or "shield" between themselves and others. This gesture can be a sign of vulnerability, self-protection, or a need for personal space, especially in unfamiliar or threatening situations.
- **Disagreement or resistance**: In some cases, arm crossing may indicate a closed or oppositional attitude, as if the person is "digging in their heels" or "putting up a fight." This interpretation is more likely when the arm crossing is accompanied by other signs of tension, such as a clenched jaw, furrowed brow, or tightened lips.
- **Self-soothing or self-restraint**: For some people, arm crossing may be a self-soothing or self-regulating behavior, providing a sense of comfort, security, or control in stressful or uncertain situations. In this context, the arm crossing may be accompanied by other self-touch behaviors, such as rubbing the upper arms or hugging the torso.

- **Concentration or contemplation**: In some cases, arm crossing may simply indicate a state of deep thought, focus, or mental engagement, as the person "closes off" external distractions to concentrate on an internal process. This type of arm crossing is often more relaxed and less tense than the defensive or oppositional varieties.

It should be noted that arm crossing is not a reliable indicator of negative emotions or closed-mindedness. Some people may habitually cross their arms as a comfortable or familiar resting position, without any particular emotional significance. Additionally, certain physical factors, such as feeling cold or having poor circulation, may lead to increased arm crossing as a way of conserving body heat or relieving tension.

To accurately interpret arm crossing and other defensive postures, it's important to consider the full context of the situation, including the person's baseline behavior, their relationship to others present, and any accompanying verbal or nonverbal cues that may provide additional insights into their emotional state and intentions. By remaining open, curious, and attuned to these nuances, we can respond to defensive signals with greater empathy, skill, and rapport-building savvy.

Leg Crossing: Mirroring, Direction, and Their Connection to Comfort Levels and Attraction

Like arm crossing, leg crossing is another common body posture that can convey a range of meanings and emotions, depending on the context and the style of the cross. Some key aspects of leg crossing and their possible interpretations include:

- **Comfort and relaxation**: In general, crossing the legs while seated is seen as a sign of comfort, ease, and informality, especially when the cross is loose, relaxed, and unforced. This type of leg crossing may indicate that the person feels safe, accepted, and at ease in their surroundings, and is not experiencing any significant stress, tension, or threat.

- **Formality and professionalism**: In more formal or professional settings, a tighter, more controlled leg cross (such as the "ankle lock" or the "figure four" cross) may be used to signal respect, attentiveness, or adherence to social norms. This type of leg crossing is often accompanied by an upright posture, direct eye contact, and other signs of engagement and focus.
- **Defensiveness or withdrawal**: In some cases, leg crossing may be used as a defensive or withdrawing posture, similar to arm crossing. If the leg cross is tight, tense, or accompanied by other signs of discomfort (such as foot jiggling or shifting), it may indicate that the person is feeling anxious, insecure, or closed off from others.
- **Mirroring and rapport**: When two people are engaged in conversation and both cross their legs in a similar manner (e.g., both with the right leg over the left), it may be a sign of mirroring, rapport, and unconscious synchrony. This type of mutual leg crossing can indicate a sense of shared understanding, empathy, or connection between the individuals involved.
- **Attraction and interest**: In social or romantic situations, leg crossing can also be used as a subtle sign of attraction or interest, especially when combined with other flirtatious cues such as smiling, leaning in, or playing with hair. For example, a woman who crosses her legs toward a man while also maintaining eye contact and laughing at his jokes may be signaling romantic interest or openness.

As with other body language cues, it's crucial to interpret leg crossing in the full context of the situation, taking into account factors such as the setting, the relationship between the individuals, and any accompanying verbal or nonverbal signals. By remaining alert to these nuances and adapting our interpretations accordingly, we can use our understanding of leg crossing and other body postures to build stronger, more authentic connections with others.

Mirroring: Building Rapport by Subtly Matching the Other Person's Body Language

Mirroring is a powerful yet often unconscious aspect of body language that involves subtly matching or mimicking the nonverbal behaviors of the person we are interacting with. When done skillfully and authentically, mirroring can help build rapport, trust, and a sense of connection between individuals, even in the absence of verbal communication.

Some key aspects of mirroring and its potential benefits include:

- **Unconscious synchrony**: Mirroring often occurs naturally and unconsciously between people who are engaged, attuned, and emotionally connected. When we feel a sense of kinship or affinity with someone, we may automatically start to match their posture, gestures, facial expressions, or vocal patterns, as a way of signaling our shared understanding and empathy.
- **Rapport and influence**: By deliberately (but subtly) mirroring the body language of others, we can create a sense of similarity, familiarity, and "togetherness" that can help build rapport, trust, and cooperation. This technique is often used by salespeople, negotiators, and other professionals who rely on interpersonal influence and persuasion to achieve their goals.
- **Emotional contagion**: Mirroring can also help create a sense of emotional contagion or "mood matching" between individuals. When we mirror someone's nonverbal cues, we may unconsciously start to feel and express similar emotions, creating a feedback loop of mutual understanding and attunement. This can be especially useful in settings such as therapy, coaching, or conflict resolution, where establishing emotional resonance is key to facilitating change and growth.
- **Cross-cultural communication**: In cross-cultural settings,

where verbal language may be a barrier, mirroring can be a powerful tool for establishing common ground and building bridges of understanding. By attuning ourselves to the unique nonverbal patterns and rhythms of a different culture, and sensitively mirroring them in our own behavior, we can demonstrate respect, open-mindedness, and a willingness to connect and learn.

To effectively use mirroring to build rapport and connection, it's important to do so subtly, gradually, and authentically. Overt or exaggerated mirroring can come across as manipulative, insincere, or even mocking, undermining the very trust and rapport we seek to build. Instead, the goal is to gently and naturally "echo" the other person's nonverbal cues, while still maintaining our own sense of individuality and personal style.

It's also important to be sensitive to the other person's reactions and adjust our mirroring accordingly. If someone seems uncomfortable, resistant, or put off by our mirroring attempts, it may be a sign that we are coming on too strong, or that there are other factors (such as power dynamics, cultural differences, or personal boundaries) that need to be respected and navigated with care.

Mirroring's power is in creating a sense of 'us' - a shared identity, understanding, and purpose that goes beyond words and connects us on a deeper, more primal level. By cultivating this skill and using it judiciously, we can tap into the fundamental human need for belonging, and build more meaningful, authentic relationships in all areas of our lives.

CHAPTER 8: POSTURE - PROJECTING CONFIDENCE AND AUTHORITY

In addition to gestures and movements, our overall body posture - the way we hold and carry ourselves in space - can convey powerful messages about our emotions, attitudes, and social status. By understanding the nonverbal cues associated with different postures, we can learn to project confidence, authority, and other desired qualities, while also reading the deeper meanings behind the postures of others.

Hunched Shoulders: Signaling Insecurity, Aloofness, or Physical Discomfort

One common posture that can convey a range of negative emotions or states is the hunched shoulder - a rounding or slumping of the upper back and shoulders, often accompanied by a lowered head and averted gaze. This posture can signal:

- **Insecurity or low self-esteem**: When someone feels unsure of themselves, anxious, or self-conscious, they may unconsciously hunch their shoulders as a way of making themselves smaller, less visible, or less threatening to others. This posture can be a sign of low confidence, self-doubt, or a desire to avoid attention or confrontation.

- **Aloofness or disengagement**: In some cases, hunched shoulders may indicate a lack of interest, involvement, or connection with others or the situation at hand. If someone is slouching, looking away, and not participating actively in a conversation or activity, it may be a sign that they are bored, distracted, or emotionally disengaged.
- **Physical discomfort or pain**: Hunched shoulders can also be a sign of physical tension, stiffness, or pain, especially in the neck, upper back, or shoulder area. If someone is constantly hunching or rolling their shoulders, rubbing their neck, or stretching their upper body, it may indicate that they are experiencing physical discomfort or stress that is affecting their posture and overall demeanor.
- **Defensiveness or self-protection**: In some situations, hunched shoulders may be a defensive or self-protective posture, similar to arm crossing or leg crossing. If someone is feeling threatened, vulnerable, or exposed, they may hunch their shoulders as a way of shielding their chest, neck, and vital organs from potential harm or attack.

To accurately interpret hunched shoulders and other closed or defensive postures, it's important to consider the full context of the situation, including the person's baseline behavior, their relationship to others present, and any accompanying verbal or nonverbal cues that may provide additional insights into their emotional state and intentions.

If someone's hunched posture seems out of character or is accompanied by other signs of discomfort, disengagement, or defensiveness, it may be a sign that they are feeling unsupported, misunderstood, or threatened in some way. In these cases, responding with empathy, curiosity, and non-judgmental listening can help create a safer, more supportive environment that encourages open communication and connection.

Shoulders Curved Forward: A Defensive Posture, Indicating Feeling Threatened

Similar to hunched shoulders, shoulders curved forward - also known as "rounded shoulders" or "slouching" - can also convey a range of defensive or self-protective emotions and attitudes. This posture involves a forward roll of the shoulders, often accompanied by a sunken chest, a lowered chin, and a curved upper back.

Some possible interpretations of shoulders curved forward include:

- **Feeling threatened or vulnerable**: When someone feels threatened, scared, or exposed, they may unconsciously curve their shoulders forward as a way of protecting their chest, neck, and vital organs. This posture can be a sign of fear, anxiety, or a heightened sense of vulnerability, especially in unfamiliar or potentially dangerous situations.
- **Lack of confidence or assertiveness**: Curved shoulders can also indicate a lack of confidence, self-assurance, or assertiveness. If someone is constantly slouching, avoiding eye contact, and speaking in a soft or hesitant voice, it may be a sign that they are unsure of themselves, their abilities, or their place in the social hierarchy.
- **Emotional pain or distress**: In some cases, shoulders curved forward may be a sign of emotional pain, sadness, or distress. If someone is going through a difficult time, grieving a loss, or feeling overwhelmed by life's challenges, they may unconsciously adopt a more closed, protective posture as a way of shielding themselves from further hurt or pain.
- **Physical fatigue or weakness**: Curved shoulders can also be a sign of physical exhaustion, weakness, or poor posture habits. If someone is constantly slouching, hunching, or leaning forward, it may indicate that they are experiencing muscle fatigue, joint pain, or other physical limitations that are affecting their ability to maintain an upright, open posture.

As with hunched shoulders, it's important to interpret curved shoulders in the full context of the situation, taking into account the person's baseline behavior, their relationship to others present, and any accompanying verbal or nonverbal cues that may provide additional insights into their emotional state and intentions.

If someone's curved shoulder posture seems out of character or is accompanied by other signs of fear, vulnerability, or emotional distress, it may be a sign that they are feeling overwhelmed, unsupported, or in need of comfort and reassurance. In these cases, responding with empathy, gentleness, and a willingness to listen and support can help create a safer, more nurturing environment that promotes healing, growth, and resilience.

Shoulders Pushed Back: Projecting Confidence, Dominance, or Power

In contrast to hunched or curved shoulders, shoulders pushed back - also known as an "open" or "expansive" posture - can convey a range of positive emotions and attitudes, such as confidence, dominance, and power. This posture involves a backward roll of the shoulders, often accompanied by an upright spine, a lifted chin, and a broad, expansive chest.

Some possible interpretations of shoulders pushed back include:

- **Confidence and self-assurance**: When someone feels confident, self-assured, and comfortable in their own skin, they may naturally adopt an open, expansive posture with their shoulders pushed back. This posture can be a sign of high self-esteem, inner strength, and a belief in one's own abilities and worth.
- **Dominance and authority**: In social or professional settings, an expansive posture with shoulders pushed back can also convey a sense of dominance, authority, or leadership. If someone is standing tall, taking up space, and projecting a commanding presence, it may be a sign that they feel in control, influential, or entitled to respect and deference from

others.

- **Openness and approachability**: Shoulders pushed back can also signal openness, friendliness, and approachability, especially when combined with other welcoming cues such as smiling, direct eye contact, and open hand gestures. This posture can be a way of inviting others in, creating a sense of warmth and connection, and demonstrating a willingness to engage and interact.
- **Resilience and determination**: In some cases, an expansive posture with shoulders pushed back may be a sign of resilience, determination, or a refusal to be cowed or intimidated by challenges or adversity. If someone is facing a difficult situation with their head held high and their shoulders back, it may indicate that they are drawing on inner reserves of strength, courage, and perseverance to overcome obstacles and achieve their goals.

As with other postures, it's important to interpret shoulders pushed back in the full context of the situation, taking into account the person's baseline behavior, their relationship to others present, and any accompanying verbal or nonverbal cues that may provide additional nuance or meaning.

While an expansive, confident posture can be a powerful tool for projecting authority, building rapport, and commanding respect, it's important to use it judiciously and authentically. Overly exaggerated or aggressive displays of dominance or entitlement can backfire, creating resentment, resistance, or even hostility in others.

Instead, the goal is to cultivate a sense of genuine confidence, openness, and respect - both for oneself and for others - that naturally manifests in an upright, expansive posture. By embodying these qualities from the inside out, we can inspire trust, admiration, and cooperation in those around us, and create a more positive, empowering social dynamic for all involved.

Shrugging: Expressing Uncertainty, Lack of Understanding, or Possible Deception

Shrugging - the act of briefly raising and lowering one's shoulders - is a common nonverbal gesture that can convey a range of meanings and emotions, depending on the context and the manner in which it is done. Some possible interpretations of shrugging include:

- **Uncertainty or lack of knowledge**: One of the most common meanings of a shrug is to express uncertainty, doubt, or a lack of knowledge about a particular topic or question. If someone is asked for information or an opinion that they don't have or aren't sure about, they may shrug their shoulders as a way of saying "I don't know" or "I'm not sure."
- **Indifference or lack of concern**: In some cases, a shrug may indicate a lack of interest, investment, or concern about a particular issue or outcome. If someone is presented with a choice or a challenge that they don't feel strongly about either way, they may shrug their shoulders as a way of saying "It doesn't matter to me" or "I don't really care."
- **Helplessness or lack of control**: A shrug can also be a sign of helplessness, powerlessness, or a lack of control over a particular situation or outcome. If someone is faced with a problem or obstacle that they feel unable to solve or overcome, they may shrug their shoulders as a way of saying "There's nothing I can do" or "It's out of my hands."
- **Possible deception or evasion**: In some cases, a shrug - especially if it is exaggerated, prolonged, or accompanied by other signs of discomfort or inconsistency - may be a sign of deception, evasion, or an attempt to avoid answering a question or taking responsibility for something. If someone is asked a direct question and responds with a noncommittal shrug, it may indicate that they are being intentionally vague, misleading, or withholding information.

As with other nonverbal gestures, it's important to interpret shrugging in the full context of the situation, taking into account the person's baseline behavior, their relationship to others present, and any accompanying verbal or nonverbal cues that may provide additional insights into their true thoughts and feelings.

If someone's shrugging seems out of character, excessive, or inconsistent with their words or other nonverbal signals, it may be a sign that they are feeling uncomfortable, evasive, or conflicted in some way. In these cases, responding with gentle curiosity, open-ended questions, and a non-judgmental attitude can help create a safe space for more honest, authentic communication and connection.

At the same time, it's important to remember that shrugging is a common and often unconscious gesture that may not always carry deep or significant meaning. Sometimes a shrug is just a shrug - a momentary expression of uncertainty, nonchalance, or a lack of strong opinion either way.

CHAPTER 9: BREATHING - THE RHYTHM OF EMOTIONS

Breathing is a fundamental biological process that is essential for life, but it is also a powerful nonverbal cue that can reveal a great deal about a person's emotional state, level of arousal, and even their underlying health and well-being. By learning to observe and interpret the subtle changes in someone's breathing patterns, we can gain valuable insights into their inner world and respond with greater sensitivity, empathy, and skill.

Deep Breathing: Excitement, Attraction, Anger, Fear, or Love

One of the most noticeable and significant changes in breathing patterns is deep breathing - a marked increase in the depth and intensity of inhalation and exhalation, often accompanied by a quickening of the breath and a rising and falling of the chest or abdomen. Deep breathing can indicate a range of heightened emotional states, such as:

- **Excitement or anticipation**: When we are looking forward to something pleasurable, such as a thrilling experience, a delicious meal, or a long-awaited reunion with a loved one, our breathing may become deeper and more rapid as a way of preparing our body for action and increasing our level of arousal and engagement.

- **Attraction or sexual arousal**: Deep breathing can also be a sign of physical attraction or sexual arousal, especially when combined with other nonverbal cues such as dilated pupils, flushed skin, and a focus on the object of desire. In intimate situations, a quickening of the breath and a deepening of inhalation can signal a heightened state of excitement, anticipation, and readiness for connection.
- **Anger or aggression**: In some cases, deep breathing may indicate a state of anger, frustration, or aggression, especially if it is accompanied by other signs of tension such as clenched fists, a tightened jaw, or flared nostrils. In these situations, the increased oxygen intake may be a way of preparing the body for a potential fight or confrontation.
- **Fear or anxiety**: Deep breathing can also be a sign of fear, anxiety, or panic, especially if it is rapid, shallow, and accompanied by other signs of distress such as trembling, sweating, or a racing heartbeat. In these cases, the heightened breathing may be a way of trying to calm or regulate the body's stress response, even as the mind is grappling with a perceived threat or danger.
- **Love or deep connection**: Finally, deep breathing can be a sign of intense love, affection, or emotional connection, especially in intimate or vulnerable moments with a romantic partner or close family member. In these situations, the synchronized and resonant breathing of two people can create a sense of unity, attunement, and shared experience that transcends words.

It's important to interpret deep breathing in the full context of the situation, taking into account the person's baseline behavior, their relationship to others present, and any accompanying verbal or nonverbal signals that may provide additional nuance or meaning.

If someone's deep breathing seems out of character or is

accompanied by other signs of strong emotion or physiological arousal, it may be a sign that they are experiencing a significant shift in their internal state that warrants further attention or response. In these cases, taking a moment to check in, offer support, or create space for expression and reflection can help foster a sense of safety, understanding, and connection.

Deep breathing is a natural and often unconscious response to a variety of stimuli and situations, and may not always show a particular emotion or intention. As with all aspects of nonverbal communication, the key is to remain curious, attuned, and open to multiple interpretations, while using our understanding of breathing patterns as one piece of a larger puzzle in decoding the rich complexities of human experience.

Sighing: Hopelessness, Sadness, or Relief

Another common and often overlooked breathing cue is sighing - a deep, audible exhalation that is often accompanied by a release of tension or a slumping of the shoulders. Sighing can convey a range of emotions and states, such as:

- **Sadness or melancholy**: One of the most common reasons for sighing is a sense of sadness, grief, or melancholy, especially when confronted with a loss, disappointment, or difficult life circumstance. In these cases, the sigh may be a way of releasing pent-up emotion, acknowledging the weight of the situation, or signaling a need for comfort or support.
- **Hopelessness or despair**: Sighing can also be a sign of hopelessness, helplessness, or despair, especially when faced with a seemingly insurmountable obstacle or challenge. In these situations, the sigh may indicate a sense of resignation, defeat, or a lack of belief in one's ability to change or improve the situation.
- **Boredom or disinterest**: In some cases, sighing may be a sign of boredom, disinterest, or a lack of engagement with

the task or conversation at hand. If someone is consistently sighing, yawning, or displaying other signs of restlessness or disengagement, it may be a signal that they are not fully present or invested in the interaction.

- **Relief or release**: Finally, sighing can also be a sign of relief, release, or a letting go of tension or anxiety, especially after a period of stress or uncertainty. In these cases, the sigh may indicate a sense of resolution, completion, or a return to a more relaxed and balanced state.

It's important to interpret sighing in the full context of the situation, taking into account the person's baseline behavior, their relationship to others present, and any accompanying verbal or nonverbal cues that may provide additional insights into their emotional state and intentions.

If someone's sighing seems excessive, prolonged, or accompanied by other signs of distress or disengagement, it may be a sign that they are struggling with deeper emotional issues or unmet needs that require further exploration and support. In these cases, responding with empathy, validation, and a willingness to listen and understand can help create a safe and nurturing space for healing and growth.

Remembering that sighing is a natural and unconscious behavior that may not always have a great deal of emotional significance is crucial. Sometimes a sigh is simply a way of resetting or recalibrating the body and mind, releasing physical tension, or transitioning from one state or activity to another.

Rapid, Heavy Breathing: Fear, Anxiety, or Physical Exertion

Rapid, heavy breathing - also known as panting, gasping, or hyperventilation - is another significant breathing cue that can indicate a heightened state of emotional or physiological arousal. This type of breathing is characterized by quick, shallow inhalations and exhalations, often accompanied by a sense of urgency, tension, or distress. Some possible reasons for rapid, heavy breathing include:

- **Fear or panic**: One of the most common causes of rapid, heavy breathing is a state of intense fear, anxiety, or panic, especially when confronted with a perceived threat or danger. In these situations, the body's sympathetic nervous system is activated, triggering a "fight or flight" response that includes increased heart rate, blood pressure, and breathing rate as a way of preparing for action or escape.
- **Physical exertion or strain**: Rapid, heavy breathing can also be a sign of physical exertion, strain, or overexertion, especially during intense exercise, manual labor, or other demanding physical activities. In these cases, the increased breathing rate is a way of delivering more oxygen to the muscles and tissues, supporting the body's increased metabolic needs, and helping to regulate temperature and maintain homeostasis.
- **Emotional or psychological stress**: In some cases, rapid, heavy breathing may be a sign of emotional or psychological stress, even in the absence of a clear external threat or physical demands. For example, someone who is experiencing intense feelings of anger, frustration, or overwhelm may exhibit rapid, shallow breathing as a way of trying to cope with or release the pent-up tension and energy in their body.
- **Medical or health issues**: Finally, rapid, heavy breathing can also be a sign of underlying medical or health issues, such as asthma, allergies, respiratory infections, or cardiovascular problems. In these cases, the breathing difficulties may be chronic or episodic, and may require professional medical attention and treatment.

Interpret rapid, heavy breathing in the full context of the situation, taking into account the person's baseline behavior, their overall health and fitness level, and any accompanying verbal or nonverbal signals that may provide additional insights into their emotional or physical state.

If someone's rapid, heavy breathing seems excessive, prolonged, or accompanied by other signs of distress or discomfort, it may be a sign that they are experiencing a significant emotional or physical challenge that requires further attention or support. In these cases, responding with concern, validation, and a willingness to offer assistance or resources can help create a sense of safety, care, and connection.

Remember that rapid, heavy breathing is a natural and often adaptive response to a wide range of stimuli and demands, and may not always indicate a serious problem or crisis.

Smell and Breathing: Involuntary Reactions to Pleasant and Unpleasant Odors

In addition to emotional and physical factors, our breathing patterns can also be influenced by the presence of different smells and odors in our environment. Our sense of smell is closely linked to the limbic system in the brain, which plays a key role in regulating emotions, memory, and behavior. As a result, our breathing can change involuntarily in response to pleasant or unpleasant scents, even before we are consciously aware of them.

Some common breathing reactions to different smells include:

- **Pleasant smells**: When we encounter a pleasant smell, such as the aroma of freshly baked bread, a fragrant flower, or a beloved perfume, our breathing may become slower, deeper, and more relaxed. This response is often accompanied by a sense of pleasure, comfort, or nostalgia, as the smell triggers positive associations and memories in the brain.
- **Unpleasant smells**: On the other hand, when we encounter an unpleasant smell, such as the odor of spoiled food, chemical fumes, or bodily waste, our breathing may become more rapid, shallow, and tense. This response is often accompanied by a sense of disgust, aversion, or anxiety,

as the smell signals a potential threat or danger to our health and well-being.
- **Neutral smells**: Finally, when we encounter a neutral smell, such as the scent of a room or a familiar object, our breathing may not change significantly from its baseline pattern. This lack of response suggests that the smell is not particularly salient or meaningful to us, and does not trigger any strong emotional or physiological reactions.

Our breathing responses to various scents can be highly individual and context-dependent, based on our unique personal experiences, cultural backgrounds, and physiological sensitivities. What smells pleasant or unpleasant to one person may not have the same effect on another, and our reactions can change over time as we form new associations and memories.

Moreover, our breathing responses to smells can also be influenced by other factors, such as our current emotional state, our level of hunger or thirst, and our overall health and well-being. For example, when we are feeling stressed or anxious, we may be more sensitive to unpleasant smells and more likely to exhibit rapid, shallow breathing in response. Similarly, when we are feeling relaxed and content, we may be more open to pleasant smells and more likely to exhibit slow, deep breathing as a result.

Paying attention to a person's breathing reactions to smells, just like other nonverbal communication aspects, can offer valuable insights into their inner world and emotional landscape. By observing how someone's breathing changes in response to different scents and odors, we can gain a deeper understanding of their preferences, aversions, and underlying psychological states.

CHAPTER 10: THE CHEST AND SHOULDERS - POWER AND VULNERABILITY

The chest and shoulders are two of the most expressive and symbolically charged areas of the body, often reflecting a person's sense of power, confidence, vulnerability, or emotional state. By learning to read and interpret the nonverbal cues associated with these regions, we can gain valuable insights into someone's inner world and respond with greater sensitivity, skill, and rapport.

Chest Puffing: Displaying Confidence, Strength, or Attempting to Appear Larger

One of the most common and noticeable nonverbal cues involving the chest is "chest puffing" - the act of inhaling deeply and expanding the chest outward, often accompanied by a lifting of the chin and a straightening of the spine. This behavior can convey a range of meanings and intentions, such as:

- **Confidence and self-assurance**: When someone feels confident, self-assured, and proud of their accomplishments or abilities, they may naturally puff out their chest as a way of displaying their strength, competence, and value. This nonverbal cue is often seen in athletes after a big win, performers after a successful show, or leaders after a triumphant speech or decision.

- **Dominance and aggression**: In some cases, chest puffing may be used as a way of asserting dominance, intimidation, or aggression towards others, especially in competitive or confrontational situations. By making themselves appear larger and more imposing, the person may be trying to establish their power, control, or superiority over others.
- **Attraction and courtship**: Chest puffing can also be a nonverbal cue used in attraction and courtship, as a way of displaying one's physical fitness, genetic health, and desirability as a mate. In these contexts, the expanded chest may be accompanied by other signs of preening or self-presentation, such as adjusting clothing, flexing muscles, or striking a pose.
- **Overcompensation and insecurity**: Finally, in some cases, chest puffing may be a sign of overcompensation, insecurity, or a need to prove oneself, especially if the behavior seems exaggerated, forced, or incongruent with the person's overall demeanor or situation. In these instances, the puffed chest may be a way of masking underlying feelings of inadequacy, self-doubt, or vulnerability.

Taken with other nonverbal cues, it's important to interpret chest puffing in the full context of the situation, taking into account the person's baseline behavior, their relationship to others present, and any accompanying verbal or nonverbal signals that may provide additional nuance or meaning.

If someone's chest puffing seems authentic, congruent, and well-received by others, it may be a sign of genuine confidence, charisma, or leadership potential that can inspire and motivate those around them. On the other hand, if the behavior seems excessive, artificial, or met with resistance or discomfort from others, it may indicate a need for greater self-awareness, humility, or emotional intelligence on the part of the sender.

Ultimately, the key to interpreting and responding to chest

puffing is to approach the behavior with curiosity, empathy, and a willingness to look beyond surface-level appearances to the deeper human needs and desires that may be driving it. By seeking to understand rather than judge, we can use our knowledge of this nonverbal cue to build stronger, more authentic connections with others and ourselves.

Shoulder Slumping: Indicating Defeat, Sadness, or Low Self-Esteem

In contrast to the expanded, uplifted posture of chest puffing, shoulder slumping is a nonverbal cue that involves a drooping or rounding of the shoulders, often accompanied by a lowered head, averted gaze, and an overall sense of deflation or contraction. This behavior can convey a range of emotions and states, such as:

- **Sadness and grief**: One of the most common reasons for shoulder slumping is a deep sense of sadness, loss, or grief, especially in the face of a profound personal or interpersonal setback. In these moments, the slumped shoulders may reflect a feeling of heaviness, emptiness, or despair, as if the person is literally weighed down by their emotions.
- **Defeat and resignation**: Shoulder slumping can also be a sign of defeat, helplessness, or resignation, especially when a person has lost hope or given up on a goal, dream, or relationship. In these cases, the contracted posture may signal a sense of powerlessness, futility, or a lack of agency in the face of overwhelming obstacles or challenges.
- **Low self-esteem and insecurity**: In some instances, chronic shoulder slumping may be a reflection of low self-esteem, self-doubt, or insecurity, especially if the behavior is part of a larger pattern of self-effacement, self-criticism, or social withdrawal. In these cases, the slumped posture may be an unconscious way of making oneself smaller, less visible, or less threatening to others.
- **Physical pain or fatigue**: Finally, shoulder slumping can also be a sign of physical pain, fatigue, or exhaustion, especially

after a period of intense exertion, stress, or illness. In these cases, the drooping shoulders may be a natural response to the body's need for rest, recovery, and self-care.

If someone's shoulder slumping seems sudden, intense, or accompanied by other signs of distress or disengagement, it may be a signal that they are in need of support, validation, or a listening ear. In these moments, responding with empathy, compassion, and a willingness to be present and attuned to their needs can help create a sense of safety, connection, and emotional healing.

If someone's shoulders slump suddenly, intensely, or with other signs of distress or disengagement, it could be a sign that they need support, validation, or a listening ear. Sometimes, a temporary slump is a natural and necessary part of the ebb and flow of human emotions, and may simply require patience, understanding, and a supportive space to move through and integrate.

CHAPTER 11: APPEARANCE AND CLOTHING - THE SILENT MESSAGES WE SEND

While not always considered a form of "body language" per se, our appearance and clothing choices can send powerful nonverbal messages about our personalities, values, social roles, and emotional states. From the colors and styles we wear to the way we groom and adorn ourselves, our visual presentation is a form of self-expression that can influence how others perceive and interact with us in countless ways.

Clothing Style: Projecting Authority, Professionalism, Casualness, or Rebellion

One of the most obvious and impactful aspects of our appearance is our clothing style - the specific types, cuts, and combinations of garments we choose to wear in different contexts. Our clothing choices can convey a wide range of meanings and intentions, such as:

- **Authority and power**: Certain clothing styles, such as tailored suits, crisp dress shirts, and polished shoes, are often associated with positions of authority, leadership, and power. By dressing in these styles, individuals may be seeking to project an image of competence, credibility, and status, especially in professional or formal settings.

- **Professionalism and respect**: Similarly, clothing that is neat, modest, and appropriate for the occasion can convey a sense of professionalism, respect, and attention to detail. By dressing in a way that shows consideration for the norms and expectations of a given context, individuals may be signaling their commitment to excellence, reliability, and teamwork.
- **Casualness and approachability**: On the other hand, clothing that is more relaxed, comfortable, and informal can convey a sense of casualness, friendliness, and approachability. By dressing in a way that puts others at ease and minimizes power differentials, individuals may be seeking to create a more open, authentic, and egalitarian atmosphere.
- **Rebellion and nonconformity**: Finally, clothing that deviates from mainstream norms or expectations can be a way of expressing rebellion, nonconformity, or a unique personal identity. By wearing styles that are edgy, unconventional, or even shocking, individuals may be seeking to challenge the status quo, assert their individuality, or align themselves with countercultural movements or subcultures.

Of course, the meanings and intentions behind clothing choices are not always straightforward or universal, and can vary widely based on cultural, generational, and personal factors. What reads as "professional" in one context may be seen as "stuffy" or "uptight" in another, while what feels like a bold fashion statement to one person may be experienced as garish or offensive to someone else.

Moreover, clothing choices are not always a reliable indicator of a person's true character, abilities, or intentions. Someone who dresses in a flashy or attention-grabbing way may be deeply insecure or compensating for other perceived weaknesses, while someone who dresses in a plain or unassuming way may be a brilliant and innovative thinker.

By seeking to understand the deeper motivations and contexts behind someone's sartorial choices, we can gain a more nuanced and empathetic understanding of who they are and what they value.level impressions.

Be mindful of the messages we may be sending through our own clothing choices, and to consider how they may be impacting our relationships, interactions, and opportunities in different areas of our lives. By dressing in a way that aligns with our authentic selves and the outcomes we wish to achieve, we can use our appearance as a tool for positive self-expression, connection, and change.

Color Choice: Light Colors (Openness), Dark Colors (Sophistication), Bright Colors (Energy)

Another powerful aspect of our appearance is our choice of colors - the specific hues, shades, and combinations we wear on our bodies and accessories. Colors can evoke strong emotional responses and associations, and can convey a range of meanings and moods, such as:

- **Light colors (openness and approachability)**: Light colors, such as white, beige, and pastels, are often associated with feelings of openness, purity, and approachability. By wearing these colors, individuals may be seeking to project an image of friendliness, innocence, or transparency, especially in situations where they want to put others at ease or build trust and rapport.
- **Dark colors (sophistication and mystery)**: Dark colors, such as black, navy, and charcoal, are often associated with feelings of sophistication, formality, and mystery. By wearing these colors, individuals may be seeking to project an image of power, elegance, or depth, especially

in situations where they want to be taken seriously or command respect.
- **Bright colors (energy and creativity)**: Bright colors, such as red, yellow, and orange, are often associated with feelings of energy, enthusiasm, and creativity. By wearing these colors, individuals may be seeking to project an image of confidence, passion, or innovation, especially in situations where they want to stand out, inspire others, or think outside the box.

Of course, the meanings and effects of color choices can vary widely based on cultural, contextual, and personal factors. What feels bold and energizing to one person may be experienced as garish or overwhelming to another, while what reads as sophisticated and mysterious in one setting may come across as drab or unapproachable in a different context.

Moreover, color associations are not always universal or fixed, and can shift over time as fashions, trends, and social norms evolve. For example, while pink was once considered a masculine color associated with war and heroism, it is now more commonly associated with femininity, romance, and tenderness in many Western cultures.

It's important to be aware of the ways in which our own color choices may be influencing how others perceive and respond to us, and to consider how we can use color strategically and authentically to achieve our goals and aspirations. Whether we're dressing for a job interview, a romantic date, or a creative project, the colors we choose can be a powerful tool for self-expression, connection, and impact.

Prints and Patterns: Curved Lines (Approachability), Straight Lines (Formality)

In addition to color, the prints and patterns we wear on our clothing can also send nonverbal messages about our personalities, moods, and social roles. From bold geometrics to soft florals, the visual textures and rhythms of our garments can convey a range of meanings and associations, such as:

- **Curved lines (approachability and fluidity)**: Clothing with curved, flowing lines and organic shapes, such as paisley, polka dots, or abstract swirls, can convey a sense of approachability, playfulness, and fluidity. By wearing these patterns, individuals may be seeking to project an image of warmth, creativity, or adaptability, especially in situations where they want to put others at ease or foster a sense of connection and collaboration.
- **Straight lines (formality and structure)**: Clothing with straight, geometric lines and angular shapes, such as stripes, checks, or herringbone, can convey a sense of formality, precision, and structure. By wearing these patterns, individuals may be seeking to project an image of professionalism, discipline, or analytical thinking, especially in situations where they want to be seen as reliable, organized, or authoritative.

Of course, the meanings and effects of prints and patterns can vary widely based on cultural, contextual, and personal factors, and may be influenced by other elements of appearance such as color, scale, and overall style. For example, a bold, large-scale floral print may read as artistic and expressive in one context, while feeling busy or overwhelming in another.

Additionally, prints and patterns are not always a reliable indication of a person's true character or intentions, and may be employed to produce a desired impression or conceal underlying insecurities or challenges. For example, someone who frequently wears busy, chaotic prints may be seeking to distract from or compensate for feelings of inner turmoil or confusion.

Consider them as one data point among many, and to approach them with curiosity, nuance, and a willingness to look beyond surface-level impressions. By seeking to understand the unique ways in which individuals use visual textures and rhythms to express themselves and navigate their social worlds, we can gain a more holistic and empathetic view of the richness and diversity of human experience.

Jewelry and Accessories: Status Symbols, Personal Expression, Cultural Significance

Beyond clothing itself, the jewelry and accessories we wear can also send powerful nonverbal messages about our identities, values, and social roles. From understated pieces to bold statement items, the decorative elements we choose to adorn ourselves with can convey a range of meanings and associations, such as:

- **Status symbols**: Certain types of jewelry and accessories, such as expensive watches, designer handbags, or precious gemstones, are often associated with wealth, luxury, and high social status. By wearing these items, individuals may be seeking to project an image of success, sophistication, or exclusivity, especially in situations where they want to be seen as influential, powerful, or discriminating.
- **Personal expression**: Other types of jewelry and accessories, such as handmade or vintage pieces, quirky novelty items, or meaningful talismans, can be a form of personal expression and self-differentiation. By wearing these items, individuals may be seeking to communicate their unique personalities, interests, or life experiences, especially in situations where they want to be seen as authentic, creative, or unconventional.
- **Cultural significance**: Many types of jewelry and accessories have deep cultural or symbolic meanings, and can serve as markers of ethnic identity, religious affiliation, or social role. For example, a hijab or kippah may signify adherence to Islamic or Jewish faith traditions, while a wedding ring or nose ring may indicate marital status or cultural heritage. By wearing these items, individuals may be seeking to express their connection to and pride in their cultural roots and values.

Of course, the meanings and effects of jewelry and accessories can vary widely based on personal, social, and historical factors, and may be influenced by other elements of appearance such as material, style, and context of use. For example, a simple string of pearls may read as classic and refined in one setting, while feeling outdated or contrived in another.

Moreover, jewelry and accessories are not always a reliable indicator of a person's true character or values, and can sometimes be used to create a desired impression or compensate for underlying insecurities or limitations. For example, someone who frequently wears flashy, attention-grabbing jewelry may be seeking to distract from or overcompensate for feelings of low self-worth or social awkwardness.

Whether we're dressing for a formal event, a cultural celebration, or a casual outing, the decorative elements we choose can be a powerful tool for self-expression, connection, and impact.

CHAPTER 12: PROXEMICS - THE LANGUAGE OF SPACE

Proxemics, or the study of how we use and interpret physical space in social interactions, is a crucial aspect of nonverbal communication that can reveal a great deal about our relationships, power dynamics, and emotional states. From the distance we maintain between ourselves and others to the way we orient our bodies in space, our proxemic behavior sends powerful messages about our intentions, attitudes, and levels of comfort or discomfort.

Vertical Space: Height Positioning and Its Connection to Dominance and Submission

One important dimension of proxemics is vertical space - the way we position ourselves in relation to others in terms of height and elevation. Our vertical positioning can convey a range of meanings and power dynamics, such as:

- **Dominance and authority**: In general, individuals who occupy higher vertical positions, such as standing on a raised platform or sitting at the head of a table, are often perceived as more powerful, authoritative, and influential than those in lower positions. This association between height and dominance is deeply ingrained in our evolutionary history, as taller individuals have often been seen as stronger, more threatening, and more able to assert their will over others.

- **Submission and deference**: Conversely, individuals who occupy lower vertical positions, such as kneeling, sitting on the floor, or looking up at others from a lower vantage point, are often perceived as more submissive, deferential, and dependent on those above them. This association between lowness and submission is reinforced by cultural norms and power structures that place certain individuals or groups in subordinate roles or positions.
- **Equality and collaboration**: When individuals occupy similar vertical positions, such as sitting at the same level or standing side by side, it can convey a sense of equality, mutuality, and collaboration.

Vertical positioning is not always a reliable indicator of a person's true power or status, and can sometimes be used to create a desired impression or compensate for underlying insecurities or limitations. For example, someone who frequently seeks out elevated positions or looks down on others may be overcompensating for feelings of inadequacy or a lack of genuine authority.

By using height and elevation strategically and authentically to achieve our goals and aspirations, we can harness the power of proxemics to create more effective, meaningful, and positive connections with others.

Horizontal Space: Intimate, Personal, Social, and Public Distances

Another key dimension of proxemics is horizontal space - the physical distance we maintain between ourselves and others in social interactions. According to anthropologist Edward T. Hall, who first coined the term "proxemics" in the 1960s, there are four main zones of interpersonal distance that we use to regulate our social behavior and communicate our relationships and intentions:

- **Intimate distance (0-18 inches)**: This is the closest zone of interpersonal space, reserved for intimate interactions with romantic partners, close family members, and trusted friends. At this distance, individuals can easily touch, hug, or whisper to each other, and may share a sense of emotional and physical closeness and vulnerability.

- **Personal distance (18 inches - 4 feet)**: This is the zone of interpersonal space used for casual interactions with friends, acquaintances, and colleagues. At this distance, individuals can easily talk and make eye contact, but are not close enough to touch or invade each other's personal space. This zone allows for a sense of personal connection and engagement, while still maintaining a degree of physical and emotional boundaries.
- **Social distance (4-12 feet)**: This is the zone of interpersonal space used for more formal or impersonal interactions, such as business meetings, classroom lectures, or public speeches. At this distance, individuals can communicate easily and effectively, but are not close enough to engage in more intimate or personal behaviors. This zone allows for a sense of social connection and participation, while still maintaining a degree of professional or interpersonal distance.
- **Public distance (12-25 feet or more)**: This is the zone of interpersonal space used for large-scale public events or interactions, such as rallies, concerts, or performances. At this distance, individuals are far enough away from each other to feel anonymous and detached, but close enough to participate in a shared experience or activity. This zone allows for a sense of collective identity and energy, while still maintaining a high degree of personal space and autonomy.

Of course, the boundaries and meanings of these proxemic zones can vary widely based on cultural, situational, and personal factors, and may be influenced by other elements of nonverbal communication such as eye contact, facial expressions, and body language. For example, in some cultures, such as Latin America or the Middle East, personal space tends to be smaller and more fluid than in North America or Northern Europe, and individuals may feel more comfortable standing or sitting closer to each other in social interactions.

Moreover, proxemic behavior is not always a reliable indicator of a person's true feelings or intentions, and can sometimes be used to create a desired impression or navigate complex social situations. For example, someone who maintains a greater distance from others may be seen as aloof or unfriendly, but may actually be feeling shy, anxious, or respectful of others' personal space.

Invading Personal Space: Reactions and Interpretations in Different Contexts

While respecting others' personal space is generally considered a basic social norm, there are times when individuals may intentionally or unintentionally invade others' proxemic boundaries, leading to a range of reactions and interpretations depending on the context and the relationship between the parties involved. Some common examples of personal space invasions and their potential meanings include:

- **Aggression and intimidation**: In some cases, invading someone's personal space can be a form of aggression, dominance, or intimidation, especially if it is done suddenly, forcefully, or without consent. For example, a bully who gets in someone's face, a boss who stands too close to an employee, or a stranger who grabs someone's arm can all be seen as threatening or disrespectful, and may elicit feelings of fear, anger, or defensiveness in the person whose space is being violated.
- **Intimacy and affection**: In other cases, invading someone's personal space can be a way of expressing intimacy, affection, or desire, especially if it is done gradually, gently, and with mutual consent. For example, a couple who leans in close to each other, a parent who hugs a child, or friends who

sit shoulder-to-shoulder can all be seen as signs of closeness, warmth, and emotional connection, and may elicit feelings of comfort, security, and belonging in the individuals involved.

- **Cultural differences**: As mentioned earlier, cultural norms and expectations around personal space can vary widely, and what is considered an appropriate or inappropriate invasion of space in one culture may be seen differently in another. For example, in some Asian cultures, it is common for people to stand very close to each other in public spaces, while in some Nordic cultures, individuals tend to maintain a greater distance and value their personal space more highly. Understanding and respecting these cultural differences is crucial for building positive relationships and avoiding misunderstandings or offense.
- **Contextual factors**: The meaning and appropriateness of personal space invasions can also depend on the specific context and situation in which they occur. For example, in a crowded elevator or subway car, it may be unavoidable and socially acceptable to stand very close to strangers, while in a formal business meeting or a doctor's office, maintaining a greater distance may be seen as more professional and respectful. Similarly, the same proxemic behavior may be interpreted differently depending on the age, gender, status, and relationship of the individuals involved.

The key to managing personal space invasions is to be aware of other people's nonverbal cues and reactions and to modify your own actions accordingly. If someone seems uncomfortable, anxious, or defensive when their space is invaded, it may be a sign to back off or apologize, while if they seem receptive, engaged, or even inviting, it may be a sign to continue or deepen the interaction.

PART 3: ADVANCED

SARAH THOMPSON

TECHNIQUES AND APPLICATIONS

CHAPTER 13: DETECTING DECEPTION - UNMASKING THE LIES

One of the most challenging and high-stakes applications of nonverbal communication is the detection of deception - the ability to identify when someone is lying, withholding information, or trying to mislead us. While no single nonverbal cue or behavior is a foolproof indicator of deception, there are certain patterns and clusters of cues that can suggest that someone is being less than truthful, and that can help us make more informed decisions and judgments in our personal and professional lives.

Why People Lie: White Lies, Social Lies, Malicious Lies

Before we can effectively detect deception, it's important to understand the different types and motivations of lies that people tell. While all lies involve a deliberate attempt to mislead or deceive, they can vary widely in their intent, severity, and consequences, and may be driven by a range of psychological, social, and situational factors. Some common types of lies include:

- **White lies**: These are harmless or even well-intentioned lies that are told to avoid hurting someone's feelings, to maintain social harmony, or to protect someone's privacy or dignity. Examples might include telling a friend that their new haircut looks great even if you don't like it, or telling a coworker that you're busy with a project when you just don't feel like socializing. While white lies are generally considered acceptable in moderation, they can still erode trust and authenticity if used too frequently or carelessly.

- **Social lies**: These are lies that are told to navigate complex social situations, to maintain appearances or reputations, or to avoid uncomfortable or awkward interactions. Examples might include exaggerating one's accomplishments or experiences to impress others, pretending to agree with someone's opinions to avoid conflict, or making excuses to get out of unwanted social obligations. While social lies can sometimes serve a useful purpose in smoothing over rough patches in relationships, they can also create a false or inauthentic sense of self and others, and can backfire if discovered or exposed.

- **Malicious lies**: These are lies that are told with the deliberate intent to harm, deceive, or manipulate others for personal gain or advantage. Examples might include lying on a job application or resume, cheating on a test or assignment, falsely accusing someone of a crime or misconduct, or deliberately spreading rumors or misinformation to damage someone's reputation or credibility. Malicious lies are generally considered the most serious and unethical form of deception, as they violate fundamental principles of honesty, integrity, and respect for others, and can have serious legal, financial, and personal consequences if exposed.

Of course, not all lies fit neatly into these categories, and people may tell different types of lies in different contexts or for different reasons. Moreover, the line between acceptable and unacceptable lying can be blurry and subjective, and can depend on factors such as the relationship between the parties involved, the potential consequences of the lie, and the cultural or social norms around honesty and deception.

The key to detecting deception is not to assume that all lies are malicious or unethical, but rather to be attuned to the specific nonverbal cues and behaviors that can suggest that someone is being less than truthful, and to use that information to guide one's judgments and decisions in a thoughtful and nuanced way.

Common Deception Cues: Eye Contact Avoidance, Restricted Body Movement, Involuntary Cover-Ups

While no single nonverbal cue or behavior is a guaranteed sign of deception, there are certain patterns and clusters of cues that have been shown to be more common in people who are lying or withholding information. Some of the most widely recognized and researched deception cues include:

- **Eye contact avoidance**: One of the most well-known and widely believed deception cues is the avoidance of eye contact - the idea that liars will look away, blink more frequently, or have "shifty eyes" when confronted with a direct question or accusation. While there is some truth to this idea, research has shown that the relationship between eye contact and deception is more complex and context-dependent than most people realize. In some cases, liars may actually maintain more eye contact than usual in an attempt to appear honest and convincing, while in other cases, they may avoid eye contact out of nervousness, shame, or discomfort, rather than deliberate deception.
- **Restricted body movement**: Another common deception cue is the restriction or freezing of body movement - the idea that liars will try to minimize or control their nonverbal behavior in order to avoid giving away their true thoughts or feelings. This might involve keeping their hands still, avoiding gestures or illustrations, or maintaining a rigid or unnatural posture. While this cue can sometimes be a sign of deception, it can also be a sign of nervousness, anxiety,

or self-consciousness, especially in high-stakes or unfamiliar situations.
- **Involuntary cover-ups**: A third common deception cue is the use of involuntary or unconscious "cover-up" behaviors - the idea that liars will unconsciously try to hide or obscure parts of their face or body that might reveal their true emotions or intentions. This might involve covering the mouth or eyes, touching the nose or neck, or playing with hair or clothing. While these behaviors can sometimes be a sign of deception, they can also be a sign of discomfort, self-soothing, or a desire for privacy or personal space.

It's important to note that none of these cues, on their own, are definitive proof of deception, and that they must be interpreted in the larger context of the individual's baseline behavior, the specific situation or interaction, and the presence or absence of other nonverbal and verbal cues. Moreover, even the most skilled and experienced lie detectors are not infallible, and can sometimes be fooled by skilled or pathological liars who have learned to control or manipulate their nonverbal behavior.

That said, by being attuned to these and other common deception cues, and by approaching the detection of deception with a critical and nuanced eye, we can increase our chances of identifying when someone is being less than truthful, and make more informed and effective decisions in our personal and professional lives. Whether we're dealing with a coworker who is falsely taking credit for a project, a partner who is cheating or hiding something, or a salesperson who is making exaggerated or misleading claims, the ability to detect deception can be a powerful tool for protecting ourselves and others from harm and exploitation.

Verbal and Nonverbal Inconsistencies: Contradictions, Timing Discrepancies, Unnatural Gestures

In addition to specific nonverbal cues or behaviors, another important aspect of detecting deception is the identification of inconsistencies or discrepancies between a person's verbal and nonverbal communication. When someone is lying or withholding information, there is often a mismatch or disconnect between what they are saying and what their body language is conveying, which can be a red flag for deception. Some common types of verbal and nonverbal inconsistencies include:

- **Contradictions**: One of the most obvious and telling signs of deception is when someone's words and actions directly contradict each other - for example, when they say "yes" while shaking their head "no," or when they claim to be happy or excited while displaying a flat or negative facial expression. These types of contradictions can suggest that the person is not being truthful or authentic, and that their nonverbal behavior is "leaking" their true thoughts or feelings.
- **Timing discrepancies**: Another common type of inconsistency is when there is a mismatch or delay between a person's verbal and nonverbal responses - for example, when they take a long pause before answering a question, or when their facial expressions or gestures lag behind their words. These types of timing discrepancies can suggest that the person is struggling to come up with a convincing or coherent response, or that they are trying to buy time to fabricate or manipulate the truth.
- **Unnatural gestures**: A third type of inconsistency is when a person's nonverbal behavior seems exaggerated, forced, or unnatural in relation to their words or the context of the interaction - for example, when they use overly emphatic or repetitive gestures, or when their facial expressions seem fake or insincere. These types of unnatural gestures can suggest that the person is trying too hard to convince or persuade, or that they are overcompensating for their lack of genuine emotion or conviction.

Of course, as with specific deception cues, these types of

inconsistencies must be interpreted with caution and in the larger context of the individual's baseline behavior and the specific situation or interaction. Not all inconsistencies are necessarily signs of deception, and some people may naturally have more expressive or animated nonverbal styles that can be mistaken for inauthenticity or exaggeration.

Moreover, even the most skilled lie detectors can sometimes be fooled by skilled or pathological liars who have learned to control or manipulate their verbal and nonverbal behavior to create a false sense of consistency or sincerity. In some cases, liars may even use their knowledge of deception cues and inconsistencies to their advantage, by deliberately displaying "honest" behaviors or avoiding "deceptive" ones in order to appear more credible or trustworthy.

By being attuned to the subtle and overt ways in which people's words and actions can diverge or contradict each other, we can increase our chances of identifying when someone is being less than truthful, and make more informed and effective decisions in our personal and professional lives.

Gaslighting: Manipulating Perceptions and Undermining Self-Confidence

One particularly insidious and damaging form of deception is gaslighting - a psychological manipulation tactic in which the deceiver deliberately tries to undermine the victim's sense of reality, memory, and self-confidence, in order to gain power and control over them. Gaslighting can take many forms, but often involves a combination of verbal and nonverbal tactics designed to confuse, disorient, and destabilize the victim, such as:

- **Denying or rewriting reality**: A key tactic of gaslighting is the denial or rewriting of objective reality - for example, when the deceiver claims that something the victim clearly remembers did not actually happen, or when they provide a false or distorted version of events that contradicts the victim's own perceptions or experiences. By constantly questioning or invalidating the victim's sense of reality, the gaslighter can create a sense of self-doubt and confusion that makes the victim more vulnerable to manipulation and control.

- **Trivializing or minimizing feelings**: Another common gaslighting tactic is the trivialization or minimization of the victim's emotions and experiences - for example, when the deceiver tells the victim that they are "overreacting" or "being too sensitive" in response to hurtful or abusive behavior, or when they dismiss the victim's concerns or needs as unimportant or invalid. By constantly undermining the victim's emotional reality and sense of self-worth, the gaslighter can create a sense of helplessness and dependence that makes the victim more susceptible to their influence and control.

- **Using nonverbal cues to create doubt**: In addition to verbal tactics, gaslighters may also use nonverbal cues and behaviors to create a sense of uncertainty or self-doubt in the victim - for example, by giving them disapproving or dismissive looks, by sighing or rolling their eyes in response to the victim's statements or questions, or by using sarcastic or condescending tones of voice. These types of nonverbal cues can be particularly powerful and insidious, as they can convey a sense of judgment or disapproval without the need for explicit words or accusations.

The effects of gaslighting can be devastating and long-lasting, as they can erode the victim's sense of self, agency, and trust in their own perceptions and judgments. Victims of gaslighting may experience a range of negative psychological and emotional consequences, such as anxiety, depression, self-doubt, and a sense of powerlessness or hopelessness. They may also have difficulty forming healthy relationships or trusting their own instincts and decisions, even long after the gaslighting has ended.

Detecting and confronting gaslighting can be particularly

challenging, as the tactics used by gaslighters are often subtle, insidious, and designed to create confusion and self-doubt. Moreover, gaslighters may be skilled at manipulating others' perceptions and impressions, and may have a network of enablers or allies who reinforce their false narratives or dismiss the victim's concerns.

That said, there are some common signs and patterns of gaslighting that can help victims and bystanders identify and resist this form of manipulation, such as:

- Constant denial or rewriting of reality, even in the face of clear evidence or corroboration
- Persistent invalidation or minimization of the victim's feelings, needs, or experiences
- Use of nonverbal cues and behaviors to convey disapproval, judgment, or superiority
- Attempts to isolate the victim from supportive friends, family, or resources
- Blaming the victim for the abusive or manipulative behavior, or casting them as the "real" problem

If you suspect that you or someone you know is being gaslighted, it's important to seek support and validation from trusted sources, such as friends, family, or mental health professionals. It's also important to document any instances of gaslighting or abuse, and to set clear boundaries and consequences for unacceptable behavior.

To combat gaslighting, it's crucial to trust your own perceptions, feelings, and experiences, and to surround yourself with individuals and resources that affirm and support your sense of reality and self-worth. By being attuned to the signs and tactics of gaslighting, and by building a strong foundation of self-awareness and self-compassion, you can protect yourself and others from this insidious form of manipulation, and cultivate healthier, more authentic relationships in all areas of your life.

CHAPTER 14: PERSONALITY TYPES - UNDERSTANDING UNDERLYING MOTIVATIONS

Another important aspect of reading people effectively is understanding the different personality types and traits that can influence their nonverbal behavior, communication style, and underlying motivations. While there are many different models and frameworks for categorizing personality types, one of the most widely used and researched is the Big Five personality traits, also known as the OCEAN model.

The Big Five Personality Traits: Openness, Conscientiousness, Extraversion, Agreeableness, Neuroticism

The Big Five personality traits are a set of five broad dimensions that describe the basic structure and variation of human personality. These traits are:

1. **Openness to experience**: This trait describes a person's willingness to try new things, explore novel ideas, and embrace change and uncertainty. People high in openness tend to be creative, curious, and open-

minded, while those low in openness tend to be more conventional, cautious, and resistant to change.
2. **Conscientiousness**: This trait describes a person's level of organization, self-discipline, and dependability. People high in conscientiousness tend to be hardworking, responsible, and detail-oriented, while those low in conscientiousness tend to be more spontaneous, flexible, and prone to procrastination.
3. **Extraversion**: This trait describes a person's level of sociability, assertiveness, and energy. People high in extraversion tend to be outgoing, talkative, and comfortable in social situations, while those low in extraversion (also known as introverts) tend to be more reserved, reflective, and focused on their inner world.
4. **Agreeableness**: This trait describes a person's level of warmth, empathy, and cooperativeness. People high in agreeableness tend to be friendly, caring, and attuned to others' needs and feelings, while those low in agreeableness tend to be more independent, competitive, and skeptical of others' motives.
5. **Neuroticism**: This trait describes a person's level of emotional stability, anxiety, and sensitivity to stress. People high in neuroticism tend to be more reactive, anxious, and prone to negative emotions, while those low in neuroticism tend to be more calm, resilient, and emotionally stable.

While everyone exhibits all five of these traits to some degree, people tend to have a dominant or preferred style that reflects their unique combination of traits. For example, someone who is high in openness and extraversion but low in conscientiousness and neuroticism might be a creative, outgoing, and spontaneous "free spirit," while someone who is high in conscientiousness and agreeableness but low in openness and extraversion might be a reliable, supportive, and detail-oriented "helper."

Understanding these personality traits can be helpful in

reading people's nonverbal behavior and communication style, as different traits tend to be associated with different patterns of body language, facial expressions, and vocal cues. For example:

- People high in openness may have more expressive and animated facial expressions, use more hand gestures and illustrators, and be more comfortable with novelty and ambiguity in their nonverbal communication.
- People high in conscientiousness may have more controlled and precise body language, maintain better eye contact and posture, and use more formal and polite language in their interactions.
- People high in extraversion may have more energetic and expansive body language, speak louder and faster, and use more positive and engaging facial expressions and vocal tones.
- People high in agreeableness may have more open and welcoming body language, smile and nod more frequently, and use more empathetic and supportive language in their communication.
- People high in neuroticism may have more tense and anxious body language, avoid eye contact or touch, and use more negative or self-deprecating language in their interactions.

Of course, these are just general tendencies, and individual differences and situational factors can also influence how people express themselves nonverbally. Moreover, people can learn to adapt or modify their communication style to fit different contexts or goals, even if it doesn't come naturally to them.

Four Distinct Personality Groups: Reserved, Regular, Exemplary, Egocentric

In addition to the Big Five personality traits, some researchers have proposed a simplified framework for categorizing people into four distinct personality groups, based on their patterns of behavior, communication style, and social orientation. These four groups are:

1. **Reserved**: People in this group tend to be introverted, cautious, and self-contained. They may have a calm and understated communication style, prefer to work independently or in small groups, and value privacy and personal space. They may also be highly analytical, detail-oriented, and focused on facts and logic rather than emotions or social dynamics.
2. **Regular**: People in this group tend to be balanced, adaptable, and easy-going. They may have a flexible and approachable communication style, be comfortable working in a variety of settings and with different types of people, and value harmony and cooperation. They may also be skilled at reading social cues, building relationships, and finding common ground with others.
3. **Exemplary**: People in this group tend to be conscientious, achievement-oriented, and self-disciplined. They may have a polished and professional communication style, set high standards for themselves and others, and value competence and excellence. They may also be natural leaders, strategic thinkers, and skilled at managing complex projects and teams.
4. **Egocentric**: People in this group tend to be confident, assertive, and self-focused. They may have a bold and charismatic communication style, seek out attention and recognition, and value status and influence. They may also be risk-takers, visionaries, and skilled at persuading and motivating others to follow their lead.

While these four groups are not mutually exclusive, and people may exhibit traits from more than one group depending on the situation or context, they can provide a useful framework for understanding the different ways in which people approach communication, relationships, and goals.

For example, when interacting with someone who exhibits more reserved traits, it may be helpful to give them space and time to process information, avoid overwhelming them with too much social interaction or emotional intensity, and focus on concrete facts and logical arguments. When interacting with someone who exhibits more egocentric traits, it may be helpful to appeal to their sense of status and achievement, provide opportunities for them to showcase their skills and knowledge, and be prepared to negotiate and assert boundaries as needed.

Of course, as with any personality framework, it's important to use these groups as a starting point for understanding and adapting to individual differences, rather than as a rigid or deterministic label. People are complex and multifaceted, and their behavior and communication style can vary widely depending on the situation, their goals, and their relationship with others.

The key to using personality groups to read people more effectively is to approach the task with empathy, flexibility, and willingness to meet them at their own level. By being attuned to the different ways in which people express themselves and interact with others, and by adapting our own communication and behavior to build rapport and understanding, we can create more positive and productive relationships in all areas of our lives.

Adapting Reading Strategies Based on Personality Types

Once you have a basic understanding of the different personality types and traits that can influence people's nonverbal behavior and communication style, the next step is to adapt your own reading strategies and interaction style to better connect with and understand others. Here are some tips for tailoring your approach based on the personality types you encounter:

- **For reserved types**: When interacting with someone who

exhibits more introverted or cautious traits, it's important to give them space and time to process information and respond at their own pace. Avoid overwhelming them with too much social interaction or emotional intensity, and focus on building trust and rapport through one-on-one conversations, active listening, and respect for their privacy and boundaries. When reading their nonverbal cues, pay attention to subtle changes in facial expressions, body posture, and vocal tone that may indicate discomfort, hesitation, or a need for more information.

- **For regular types**: When interacting with someone who exhibits more balanced or easy-going traits, it's important to be flexible, adaptable, and attuned to their social and emotional needs. Engage them in friendly, open-ended conversations that allow for mutual sharing and understanding, and be willing to adjust your communication style to match their preferred pace and tone. When reading their nonverbal cues, pay attention to signs of engagement, rapport, and collaboration, such as mirroring, eye contact, and positive facial expressions.

- **For exemplary types**: When interacting with someone who exhibits more conscientious or achievement-oriented traits, it's important to be professional, organized, and focused on goals and outcomes. Engage them in structured, task-oriented conversations that allow for clear expectations, timelines, and deliverables, and be prepared to provide specific examples and evidence to support your ideas and proposals. When reading their nonverbal cues, pay attention to signs of interest, agreement, and motivation, such as nodding, leaning forward, and taking notes.

- **For egocentric types**: When interacting with someone who exhibits more confident or assertive traits, it's important to be direct, persuasive, and attuned to their need for recognition and influence. Engage them in energetic, visionary conversations that allow for brainstorming, risk-taking, and big-picture thinking, and be prepared to negotiate and assert boundaries as needed to maintain a balanced and mutually beneficial relationship. When reading their nonverbal cues, pay attention to signs of excitement, enthusiasm, and dominance, such as expansive gestures, animated facial expressions, and a commanding vocal presence.

It's important to remember that people are not fixed or one-dimensional, and may exhibit different personality traits and behaviors depending on their goals, emotions, and environment.

The purpose of reading people through their personality types is not to pigeonhole or stereotype them, but rather to gain a deeper understanding and appreciation of the diverse nature of human behavior and communication. By approaching each interaction with an open mind, a compassionate heart, and a willingness to learn and grow, you can use your knowledge of personality types as a powerful tool for personal and professional success.

CHAPTER 15: MOTIVES AND BEHAVIOR - DECIPHERING THE "WHY"

When reading people and trying to understand their behavior, it's important to go beyond just the "what" and "how" of their nonverbal cues and communication style, and also consider the "why" behind their actions and motivations. Understanding someone's underlying motives and drivers can provide valuable insight into their goals, values, and decision-making processes, and can help you build more effective and mutually beneficial relationships.

Maslow's Hierarchy of Needs: Understanding Basic Human Drives and Their Influence on Behavior

One well-known framework for understanding human motivation is Maslow's Hierarchy of Needs, which proposes that people have different levels of needs that influence their behavior and priorities. According to this theory, there are five main levels of needs, arranged in a pyramid from the most basic to the most advanced:

1. **Physiological needs**: These are the most basic and essential needs for survival, such as food, water, shelter, and rest. Until these needs are met, people are unlikely to

focus on higher-level needs or goals.
2. **Safety needs**: Once physiological needs are met, people seek to feel safe, secure, and protected from harm. This can include physical safety, as well as emotional and financial security.
3. **Love and belonging needs**: After safety needs are met, people seek to form and maintain relationships, feel accepted and valued by others, and be part of a community or group.
4. **Esteem needs**: Once love and belonging needs are met, people seek to develop a sense of self-worth, achievement, and recognition from others. This can include both internal sources of esteem, such as self-respect and confidence, as well as external sources, such as status and prestige.
5. **Self-actualization needs**: At the top of the pyramid, people seek to fulfill their full potential and achieve a sense of purpose, creativity, and personal growth. This can involve pursuing meaningful goals, developing new skills and knowledge, and making a positive impact on the world.

According to Maslow, people are motivated to fulfill these needs in a hierarchical order, starting with the most basic and progressing to the more advanced as each level is satisfied. However, the specific ways in which people seek to meet these needs can vary widely depending on their individual circumstances, personality, and values.

When reading people and trying to understand their behavior, it can be helpful to consider which level of needs they may be focused on at any given moment, and how this may be influencing their nonverbal cues and communication style. For example:

- Someone who is struggling to meet their physiological needs may exhibit signs of stress, fatigue, or distraction, and may be less focused on social or emotional connections.

- Someone who is focused on safety needs may exhibit more cautious or defensive body language, and may be more attuned to potential threats or risks in their environment.
- Someone who is seeking love and belonging may exhibit more open and engaging body language, and may be more focused on building and maintaining relationships with others.
- Someone who is focused on esteem needs may exhibit more confident and assertive body language, and may be more focused on achieving goals and gaining recognition from others.
- Someone who is striving for self-actualization may exhibit more creative and expressive body language, and may be more focused on personal growth and making a meaningful contribution to the world.

It should be noted that these are only general tendencies, and nonverbal behavior can be influenced by individual differences and situational factors. Moreover, people can have multiple needs and motivations operating at the same time, and may prioritize them differently depending on the context and their personal values.

By being attuned to the deeper drives and aspirations that may be influencing someone's behavior and communication style, we can gain a more nuanced understanding of their unique perspective and experience, and tailor our own interactions and support to better meet their needs and goals.

Maslow's Hierarchy of Needs is just one framework for understanding human motivation, and that there are many other factors that can influence people's behavior and decision-making, such as cultural background, personal history, and individual differences in personality and values. By remaining open and flexible in our approach to reading people, and by using multiple lenses and sources of information to inform our understanding, we can develop a more comprehensive and accurate picture of what drives and motivates others.

Experience and Context: Recognizing the Role of Personal History and Situational Factors

In addition to basic human needs and drives, people's behavior and nonverbal communication can also be heavily influenced by their personal history, experiences, and the specific context and situation they find themselves in. Understanding these factors can provide valuable insight into someone's perspective, motivations, and challenges, and can help you build more effective and empathetic relationships.

Some key aspects of experience and context to consider when reading people include:

- **Cultural background**: People's cultural upbringing and values can have a significant impact on their communication style, social norms, and expectations for behavior. For example, someone from a more individualistic culture may exhibit more assertive and direct body language, while someone from a more collectivistic culture may exhibit more subtle and indirect cues.
- **Family dynamics**: People's early experiences with family relationships and roles can shape their attachment styles, emotional regulation, and patterns of interaction with others. For example, someone who grew up in a chaotic or neglectful family environment may exhibit more anxious or avoidant body language, while someone who grew up in a supportive and nurturing family may exhibit more secure and open nonverbal cues.
- **Trauma and adversity**: People who have experienced significant trauma, loss, or adversity in their lives may exhibit different patterns of nonverbal behavior and communication than those who have had more stable and secure experiences. For example, someone who has experienced abuse or violence may exhibit more

hypervigilant or defensive body language, while someone who has experienced discrimination or marginalization may exhibit more guarded or self-protective cues.

- **Professional and social roles**: People's behavior and communication style can also be influenced by the specific roles and expectations they face in different professional and social contexts. For example, someone who is in a position of authority or leadership may exhibit more confident and assertive body language, while someone who is in a subordinate or service role may exhibit more deferential and accommodating cues.
- **Immediate situation and goals**: Finally, people's nonverbal behavior can be heavily influenced by the specific situation they are in and the goals they are trying to achieve in that moment. For example, someone who is trying to persuade or influence others may exhibit more expansive and animated body language, while someone who is trying to avoid conflict or maintain harmony may exhibit more subtle and conciliatory cues.

In the end, it's essential to keep curious, empathetic, and committed to ongoing learning and growth when using experience and context to read people more effectively. By continuously expanding our own understanding of the diverse ways in which people navigate their lives and relationships, and by using this knowledge to inform our interactions and support, we can create more positive and transformative outcomes for ourselves and others.

Identifying Selfishness vs. Altruism: Understanding the Balance of Personal Gain and Helping Others

Another important factor to consider when reading people and trying to understand their motives and behavior is the balance between selfishness and altruism - that is, the extent to which someone is driven by a desire for personal gain or a desire to help and benefit others. While most people exhibit a mix of both selfish and altruistic tendencies, understanding which motive is more dominant in a given situation can provide valuable insight into someone's goals, values, and decision-making process.

Some key indicators of selfishness vs. altruism to look for in someone's nonverbal behavior and communication style include:

- **Focus of attention**: People who are more selfish may exhibit more self-focused body language and communication, such as talking excessively about themselves, interrupting others, or failing to listen or show interest in others' perspectives. In contrast, people who are more altruistic may exhibit more other-focused cues, such as active listening, empathy, and a willingness to put others' needs and concerns before their own.
- **Emotional expression**: People who are more selfish may exhibit more negative or self-serving emotions, such as anger, frustration, or entitlement, when their personal goals or desires are thwarted. In contrast, people who are more altruistic may exhibit more positive or other-oriented emotions, such as compassion, gratitude, or a sense of shared purpose, even in challenging or stressful situations.
- **Resource allocation**: People who are more selfish may exhibit more possessive or territorial body language and behavior, such as hoarding resources, claiming credit for others' work, or refusing to share or compromise. In contrast, people who are more altruistic may exhibit more generous and collaborative cues, such as offering help or support, sharing credit and recognition, and making sacrifices for the greater good.
- **Conflict resolution**: People who are more selfish may exhibit more defensive or aggressive body language and communication during conflicts, such as blaming others, making threats, or refusing to take responsibility for their actions. In contrast, people who are more altruistic may exhibit more constructive and conciliatory cues, such as active listening, expressing empathy, and seeking win-win

solutions that benefit everyone involved.

These are just general tendencies, and there are also differences in individuals and situations that can impact how people balance their own needs and desires with those of others. Moreover, selfishness and altruism are not always mutually exclusive, and people can exhibit both tendencies in different contexts or at different times.

When reading people and trying to understand their motives and behavior, it's important to consider the full range of factors that may be influencing their actions, and to avoid making quick judgments or assumptions based on limited information. By being attuned to the subtle cues and patterns that may indicate a more selfish or altruistic orientation, and by adapting our own approach and expectations accordingly, we can build more effective and mutually beneficial relationships with others.

CHAPTER 16: SEDUCTION AND ATTRACTION - THE NONVERBAL DANCE

One of the most fascinating and complex areas of nonverbal communication is the realm of seduction and attraction - the subtle and often unconscious ways in which people express romantic or sexual interest, build rapport and desire, and navigate the delicate dance of human courtship. Whether you're looking to improve your own dating and relationship skills, or simply seeking to understand the dynamics of attraction and desire more deeply, learning to read and interpret the nonverbal cues of seduction can be a powerful tool for personal and interpersonal growth.

Getting Noticed: Subtle Strategies to Attract Attention and Spark Interest

The first step in any seduction or attraction scenario is getting noticed - catching the attention and interest of the person you're drawn to, and signaling your own availability and desirability. While this can sometimes involve overt or aggressive tactics, such as bold pickup lines or physical advances, research suggests that more subtle and indirect strategies are often more effective in sparking genuine attraction and connection.

Some key nonverbal strategies for getting noticed and attracting attention include:

- **Eye contact**: Making and holding eye contact is one of the most powerful ways to signal interest and invitation, and to create a sense of intimacy and connection. When trying to catch someone's attention, try making brief but frequent eye contact, holding their gaze for a second or two longer than usual, and then looking away with a slight smile or head tilt. This can convey a sense of curiosity, playfulness, and openness, without being too intense or aggressive.
- **Body orientation**: The way you orient your body in relation to someone else can also send powerful nonverbal messages of interest and attraction. When trying to get noticed, try angling your body towards the person you're interested in, leaning in slightly, and opening up your posture to convey a sense of receptivity and engagement. Avoid crossing your arms, turning away, or closing off your body language, which can signal disinterest or defensiveness.
- **Preening and self-touch**: Subtle forms of preening and self-touch, such as fixing your hair, adjusting your clothing, or touching your face or neck, can also be effective ways to draw attention and convey a sense of self-awareness and attractiveness. When done in a natural and tasteful way, these behaviors can signal that you're taking care of yourself and feel good about your appearance, which can be attractive and inviting to others.
- **Smiling and laughter**: Finally, smiling and laughter are powerful nonverbal cues that can help create a positive and engaging atmosphere, and signal your own sense of warmth, happiness, and approachability. When trying to get noticed, try smiling genuinely and frequently, laughing at the other person's jokes or stories, and using your facial expressions to convey a sense of joy and connection. Avoid fake or forced smiles, or laughter that seems insincere or mocking, which can be off-putting or offensive.

Of course, these strategies are not guaranteed to work in every situation, and individual differences and contextual factors can also influence how people respond to nonverbal cues of attraction and interest. Moreover, it's important to use these strategies in a respectful and consensual way, and to be attuned to the other person's own nonverbal signals and boundaries.

To get noticed and spark interest, it's important to be authentic, confident, and able to adapt to the unique dynamics of each interaction. By using subtle and indirect nonverbal cues to convey your own attractiveness and desirability, while also being sensitive and responsive to the other person's needs and preferences, you can create a sense of mutual interest and connection that can lead to deeper and more fulfilling relationships.

Mirroring: Building Rapport and Suggesting Shared Values

Once you've caught someone's attention and sparked their interest, the next step in the seduction and attraction process is building rapport and creating a sense of connection and compatibility. One powerful nonverbal strategy for achieving this is mirroring - the subtle and often unconscious mimicry of the other person's body language, facial expressions, and vocal patterns.

Research suggests that mirroring is a natural and instinctive behavior that helps create a sense of similarity, familiarity, and belonging between people. When we mirror someone else's nonverbal cues, we signal that we are attuned to their emotional state, share their values and preferences, and are interested in building a deeper connection with them.

Some key aspects of mirroring to consider when building rapport and suggesting shared values include:

- **Posture and gestures**: One of the most basic forms of

mirroring involves matching the other person's posture and gestures, such as crossing your legs or arms in the same way, leaning in or away at the same angle, or using similar hand movements and facial expressions. When done subtly and naturally, this can create a sense of synchrony and coordination between you, and signal that you are on the same wavelength and share a common understanding of the interaction.

- **Vocal patterns**: Another important aspect of mirroring involves matching the other person's vocal patterns, such as their tone, pitch, volume, and speed of speech. By adapting your own voice to mirror the other person's style and rhythm, you can create a sense of harmony and attunement, and signal that you are listening and responding to their unique needs and preferences. Avoid mimicking the other person's accent or mannerisms in a way that seems mocking or insincere, which can be off-putting or offensive.
- **Emotional expressions**: Finally, mirroring can also involve matching the other person's emotional expressions, such as smiling when they smile, frowning when they frown, or showing concern or empathy when they express sadness or frustration. By reflecting the other person's emotions back to them in a genuine and caring way, you can create a sense of emotional resonance and support, and signal that you are there for them and understand their feelings on a deep level.

Mirroring is not a strategy that works equally for everyone, as personal differences and context can play a role in how people react to nonverbal mimicry and attunement. Moreover, it's important to use mirroring in a subtle and natural way, and to avoid coming across as insincere, manipulative, or creepy.

Using mirroring effectively in seduction and attraction requires authenticity, sensitivity, and a genuine desire to connect and understand the other person. By using nonverbal cues to build rapport, suggest shared values, and create a sense of intimacy and compatibility, you can lay the foundation for a deeper and more fulfilling relationship that is based on mutual respect, trust, and affection.

At the same time, it's important to remember that mirroring is just one tool in the larger toolkit of seduction and attraction, and that true connection and intimacy require a holistic and multifaceted approach that takes into account the unique needs, preferences, and boundaries of each individual.

Vulnerability: Signaling Trust and Openness Through Body Language

Another key aspect of seduction and attraction is vulnerability - the willingness to let down one's guard, share one's true thoughts and feelings, and be open and authentic with another person. While vulnerability can feel risky and uncomfortable at times, research suggests that it is also a powerful catalyst for building trust, intimacy, and connection in relationships.

When it comes to nonverbal communication, vulnerability can be signaled through a variety of body language cues that convey a sense of openness, receptivity, and emotional accessibility. Some key indicators of vulnerability to look for in seduction and attraction scenarios include:

- **Open body posture**: One of the most basic ways to signal vulnerability through body language is to adopt an open and expansive posture, with uncrossed arms and legs, relaxed shoulders, and an exposed torso. This posture conveys a sense of confidence, approachability, and willingness to engage with others, and can be especially powerful when combined with direct eye contact and a warm, genuine smile.
- **Self-touch and self-soothing**: Another way to signal vulnerability is through subtle forms of self-touch and self-soothing, such as touching one's face, neck, or hair, or fidgeting with jewelry or clothing. These behaviors can convey a sense of nervousness, self-consciousness, or

emotional exposure, and can be especially effective in creating a sense of intimacy and shared experience with another person. However, it's important to use these cues in moderation, and to avoid coming across as overly anxious or insecure.

- **Emotional expression**: Finally, vulnerability can also be signaled through authentic and expressive emotional displays, such as tearing up when sharing a personal story, laughing freely and uninhibitedly, or showing genuine concern or empathy for another person's feelings. By allowing oneself to be emotionally open and transparent, one can create a sense of trust, connection, and mutual understanding that can be deeply attractive and compelling to others.

Embracing vulnerability isn't always easy or comfortable, and individual differences and situational factors can have an impact on how people express and respond to nonverbal cues of openness and emotional exposure. Furthermore, it is essential to be aware of one's own boundaries and comfort levels, and to avoid oversharing or becoming overly emotional at an early stage in a relationship.

To effectively use vulnerability for seduction and attraction, it's crucial to approach it with authenticity, sensitivity, and a genuine desire to connect and share oneself with another person. By using nonverbal cues to signal trust, openness, and emotional accessibility, you can create a sense of intimacy, rapport, and mutual understanding that can deepen and enrich your relationships over time.

Keeping in mind that vulnerability is not a guarantee of attraction or connection, and that true intimacy requires a foundation of mutual respect, consent, and compatibility.

Physical Contact: Escalating Intimacy and Creating a Connection

As seduction and attraction progress, physical contact often becomes an increasingly important aspect of nonverbal communication, serving to escalate intimacy, deepen connection, and signal mutual desire and affection. While the specific forms and meanings of touch can vary widely across cultural, situational, and personal contexts, there are some general principles and strategies that can be useful in navigating this delicate and powerful aspect of human interaction.

Some key considerations for using physical contact effectively in seduction and attraction include:

- **Gradual escalation**: One of the most important principles of physical contact in seduction is to start small and escalate gradually, building comfort and consent at each stage of the interaction. This might involve starting with brief, casual touches on the arm or shoulder, and progressing to more intimate forms of contact, such as holding hands, hugging, or kissing, as the relationship develops and deepens. By taking things slowly and being attuned to the other person's nonverbal cues and comfort levels, you can create a sense of safety, trust, and mutual desire that can make physical intimacy feel natural and rewarding.
- **Contextual awareness**: Another important consideration is to be aware of the social and situational context in which physical contact is taking place, and to adjust one's approach accordingly. For example, touching someone's face or hair might feel appropriate and intimate in a private, romantic setting, but could be seen as invasive or inappropriate in a professional or public context. Similarly, the meaning and appropriateness of different forms of touch can vary widely across cultural and personal boundaries, and it's important to be sensitive and respectful of these differences.
- **Nonverbal attunement**: Finally, effective physical contact in seduction and attraction requires a high degree of nonverbal attunement and sensitivity, both to one's

own bodily sensations and emotions, and to the cues and responses of the other person. This might involve paying attention to subtle changes in breathing, muscle tension, or skin temperature, as well as to more overt signs of pleasure, discomfort, or arousal. By being fully present and responsive in the moment, and by communicating openly and honestly about one's own desires and boundaries, you can create a sense of mutual trust, respect, and connection that can make physical intimacy feel safe, consensual, and deeply fulfilling.

It's not always easy or straightforward to have physical contact, and individual differences and personal histories can affect how individuals feel and express intimacy and desire. Moreover, it's important to be mindful of issues of power, consent, and safety, and to avoid using touch in ways that feel coercive, manipulative, or disrespectful.

The most important aspect of effective physical contact in seduction and attraction is to treat it with care, sensitivity, and a deep respect for the autonomy and well-being of everyone involved. By using nonverbal cues to escalate intimacy gradually, build trust and consent, and create a sense of mutual connection and pleasure, you can cultivate more authentic and fulfilling sexual and romantic relationships that are based on genuine care, communication, and mutual understanding.

CHAPTER 17: INFLUENCING OTHERS - THE POWER OF NONVERBAL PERSUASION

In addition to building rapport, trust, and connection, nonverbal communication can also be a powerful tool for influencing and persuading others in a variety of personal and professional contexts. Whether you're trying to sell a product, pitch an idea, or motivate a team, understanding how to use body language, facial expressions, and other nonverbal cues effectively can give you a significant advantage in achieving your goals and making a positive impact on others.

Projecting Confidence and Authority Through Posture

One of the most fundamental ways to influence others through nonverbal communication is by projecting confidence and authority through your posture and body language. Research has shown that people who exhibit an upright, expansive, and relaxed posture are often perceived as more competent, trustworthy, and persuasive than those who appear slouched, tense, or withdrawn.

Some key strategies for using posture to project confidence and authority include:

- **Stand tall**: Maintaining an upright and elongated spine, with your shoulders back and your chest open, can convey a sense of strength, poise, and self-assurance. This posture not only makes you appear more confident and capable, but can also help you feel more empowered and energized from the inside out.
- **Take up space**: Adopting an expansive and open posture, with your arms and legs uncrossed and your body taking up a comfortable amount of space, can signal dominance, assertiveness, and a willingness to engage with others. This can be especially effective when combined with direct eye contact and a warm, genuine smile.
- **Use purposeful gestures**: Incorporating deliberate and expressive gestures into your communication, such as pointing, emphasizing key words with hand movements, or using open-palm gestures to convey honesty and sincerity, can help you appear more authoritative, passionate, and persuasive. However, it's important to use gestures in moderation and to avoid overdoing them, which can come across as forced or insincere.
- **Maintain composure**: Finally, projecting confidence and authority through your posture also involves maintaining a sense of calm, control, and emotional stability, even in the face of challenges or setbacks. This might involve taking deep breaths, relaxing your facial muscles, and keeping your movements smooth and deliberate, rather than rushed or erratic.

Of course, confidence and authority are not just about posture, and it's important to cultivate these qualities from the inside out, through a combination of self-awareness, self-care, and continuous learning and growth. Moreover, it's important to use these nonverbal cues in a way that feels authentic and congruent with your own personality and values, rather than trying to force yourself into a mold that doesn't fit.

By aligning your body language with your inner state and your external goals, you can create a powerful sense of presence and influence that can inspire and motivate others to follow your lead.

Building Trust Through Open Body Language and Genuine Smiles

Another key aspect of nonverbal influence and persuasion is building trust and rapport with others through open and authentic body language and facial expressions. Research has shown that people are more likely to be influenced by those they perceive as warm, sincere, and trustworthy, and that nonverbal cues play a crucial role in conveying these qualities.

Some key strategies for building trust through open body language and genuine smiles include:

- **Maintain an open posture**: Adopting an open and relaxed posture, with your arms and legs uncrossed and your body turned towards the other person, can signal approachability, receptivity, and a willingness to engage and connect. This can help create a sense of safety and comfort that can foster trust and openness in the interaction.
- **Use genuine smiles**: Smiling is one of the most powerful nonverbal cues for building trust and rapport, as it can convey warmth, friendliness, and positive regard for the other person. However, it's important to use genuine smiles that involve both the mouth and the eyes (the so-called "Duchenne smile"), rather than forced or insincere smiles that can come across as manipulative or untrustworthy.
- **Show active listening**: Another key way to build trust through body language is to demonstrate active listening and engagement with the other person, through nonverbal cues such as nodding, leaning in, and maintaining eye contact. This can help convey a sense of interest, empathy, and respect for the other person's thoughts and feelings, and can encourage them to open up and share more fully.

- **Use touch strategically**: Finally, using touch strategically and appropriately can also be a powerful way to build trust and rapport, by creating a sense of connection, comfort, and shared experience. This might involve a light touch on the arm or shoulder, a handshake, or a hug, depending on the context and the relationship between the individuals. However, it's important to use touch in a way that feels natural, consensual, and respectful of the other person's boundaries and preferences.

Of course, building trust through nonverbal communication is not a one-time event, but an ongoing process that requires consistency, authenticity, and a genuine commitment to the well-being and success of others. Moreover, it's important to be aware of individual and cultural differences in nonverbal communication styles and preferences, and to adjust one's approach accordingly.

Ultimately, the key to building trust through open body language and genuine smiles is to approach it with authenticity, empathy, and a deep respect for the autonomy and dignity of all involved. By using nonverbal cues to convey warmth, sincerity, and positive regard, you can create a foundation of trust and rapport that can facilitate more effective communication, collaboration, and influence in all areas of your life.

At the same time, it's important to remember that trust is a two-way street, and that building authentic relationships requires vulnerability, reciprocity, and a willingness to listen and learn from others. By remaining open, curious, and committed to mutual growth and understanding, we can use our knowledge of nonverbal influence to create more meaningful, impactful, and transformative connections with ourselves and others.

Mirroring and Matching for Enhanced Rapport

As discussed earlier in the context of seduction and attraction, mirroring and matching are powerful nonverbal techniques for building rapport, creating a sense of similarity and connection, and enhancing one's ability to influence and persuade others. By subtly and strategically mimicking the body language, facial expressions, and vocal patterns of the person you're interacting with, you can create a sense of unconscious alignment and attunement that can make them more receptive to your ideas and suggestions.

Some key strategies for using mirroring and matching effectively in influence and persuasion include:

- **Match posture and gestures**: One of the most basic forms of mirroring involves matching the other person's posture and gestures, such as crossing your legs or arms in the same way, leaning in or away at the same angle, or using similar hand movements and facial expressions. When done subtly and naturally, this can create a sense of synchrony and coordination that can enhance rapport and trust.
- **Mirror vocal patterns**: Another important aspect of mirroring involves matching the other person's vocal patterns, such as their tone, pitch, volume, and speed of speech. By adapting your own voice to mirror their style and rhythm, you can create a sense of harmony and attunement that can make them feel heard, understood, and valued.
- **Use strategic pacing**: In addition to matching the other person's nonverbal cues, you can also use mirroring and matching strategically to pace and lead the interaction in a desired direction. For example, you might start by mirroring their body language and vocal patterns to build rapport, and then gradually shift your own nonverbals to guide them towards a more open, engaged, or receptive state.
- **Be authentic and respectful**: Finally, it's important to use mirroring and matching in a way that feels authentic, respectful, and congruent with your own personality and values. Avoid mimicking the other person in a way that feels forced, insincere, or manipulative, and be sure to respect their boundaries and preferences throughout the

interaction.

Of course, mirroring and matching are not foolproof techniques, and individual differences and situational factors can also influence how people respond to nonverbal mimicry and attunement. Moreover, it's important to be aware of power dynamics and cultural differences that may affect the appropriateness and effectiveness of these techniques in different contexts.

To successfully use mirroring and matching in influence and persuasion, it's important to approach it with sensitivity, flexibility, and a genuine desire to connect and collaborate with others. By using nonverbal cues to build rapport, create alignment, and guide the interaction towards a mutually beneficial outcome, you can enhance your ability to influence and inspire others in a wide range of personal and professional settings.

True influence and persuasion require more than just nonverbal techniques, and that building authentic relationships and achieving lasting impact require a holistic and multifaceted approach that takes into account the unique needs, goals, and perspectives of all involved.

Using Gestures and Eye Contact for Emphasis and Connection

Another powerful way to use nonverbal communication for influence and persuasion is through the strategic use of gestures and eye contact to emphasize key points, convey emotions and intentions, and create a sense of connection and engagement with others. Research has shown that people who use expressive and purposeful gestures and maintain appropriate levels of eye contact are often perceived as more charismatic, persuasive, and memorable than those who appear stiff, disconnected, or unengaged.

Some key strategies for using gestures and eye contact effectively in influence and persuasion include:

Use illustrative gestures: One of the most effective ways to use gestures for emphasis and clarity is to use illustrative gestures that visually represent or reinforce the content of your message. For example, you might use a sweeping hand motion to convey a sense of scale or scope, a pointing gesture to draw attention to a specific detail or example, or a rhythmic gesture to underscore the cadence and flow of your words. When used strategically and in moderation, illustrative gestures can help make your message more vivid, memorable, and persuasive.

Convey emotions through gestures: In addition to illustrating content, gestures can also be used to convey emotions and intentions that can enhance your ability to connect with and influence others. For example, you might use open-palm gestures to convey honesty and sincerity, emphatic gestures to convey passion and conviction, or expansive gestures to convey confidence and authority. By aligning your gestures with your emotional state and your intended impact, you can create a more authentic and compelling presence that can inspire and motivate others.

Maintain appropriate eye contact: Another key aspect of nonverbal influence is maintaining appropriate levels of eye contact that convey interest, engagement, and connection with others. In general, maintaining eye contact for about 60-70% of the interaction is considered optimal for building rapport and trust, while avoiding prolonged or intense eye contact that can come across as aggressive or intimidating. By varying your eye contact based on the context and the individual, and by using it strategically to emphasize key points or convey emotions, you can create a more dynamic and influential communication style.

Combine gestures and eye contact: Finally, the most powerful and effective use of nonverbal influence often involves combining gestures and eye contact in strategic and synergistic ways. For example, you might use a pointing gesture while simultaneously making direct eye contact with a specific individual to draw their attention and emphasize a key point. Or you might use an expansive gesture while sweeping your gaze across the room to create a sense of inclusivity and shared experience with your audience. By coordinating your gestures and eye contact in purposeful and dynamic ways, you can create a more engaging, memorable, and persuasive communication style that can captivate and inspire others.

The key to using gestures and eye contact effectively in influence and persuasion is to approach them as tools for enhancing connection, clarity, and mutual understanding, rather than as tricks for getting your way.

To truly make a lasting impact and build meaningful relationships, cultivate a wide range of skills and capacities, including empathy, active listening, critical thinking, and emotional intelligence.

CHAPTER 18: MASTERING YOUR OWN NONVERBAL COMMUNICATION

While much of this book has focused on reading and interpreting the nonverbal cues of others, it's equally important to develop awareness and mastery of your own nonverbal communication. By understanding how your body language, facial expressions, and vocal patterns are perceived by others, and by learning to align them with your true intentions and goals, you can become a more effective, authentic, and influential communicator in all areas of your life.

Self-Awareness: Identifying and Understanding Your Personal Nonverbal Patterns

The first step in mastering your own nonverbal communication is developing greater self-awareness of your habitual patterns, tendencies, and blind spots. This involves paying close attention to your own body language, facial expressions, and vocal cues in different situations and contexts, and noticing how they may be influencing your interactions and relationships with others.

Some key strategies for increasing self-awareness of your

nonverbal communication include:

- **Observe yourself in the mirror**: One simple but powerful way to gain insight into your nonverbal patterns is to observe yourself in a mirror while engaging in different activities, such as having a conversation, giving a presentation, or expressing different emotions. Notice how your posture, gestures, facial expressions, and vocal tone shift and change in response to different stimuli, and consider how they may be perceived by others.
- **Ask for feedback from others**: Another valuable way to increase self-awareness is to seek out feedback from trusted friends, colleagues, or mentors on how your nonverbal communication is coming across. Ask them to share specific examples of times when your body language or tone of voice conveyed a particular message or emotion, and be open to their insights and suggestions for improvement.
- **Record yourself on video**: A third strategy for increasing self-awareness is to record yourself on video in different situations, such as giving a speech, participating in a meeting, or engaging in a social interaction. Review the footage carefully, paying attention to your nonverbal cues and how they may be influencing the dynamics of the interaction. Look for patterns or tendencies that may be holding you back or undermining your effectiveness, and identify areas for growth and development.
- **Practice mindfulness and self-reflection**: Finally, developing greater self-awareness of your nonverbal communication requires ongoing mindfulness and self-reflection. Take time each day to check in with yourself and notice how your body feels, what emotions you're experiencing, and how they may be manifesting in your nonverbal cues. Cultivate a curious, non-judgmental

attitude towards your own patterns and tendencies, and be willing to experiment with new ways of communicating and expressing yourself.

The process of increasing your self-awareness of your nonverbal communication is an ongoing process that demands patience, persistence, and the willingness to go beyond your comfort zone. It can be uncomfortable or even confronting to see yourself through the eyes of others, and to recognize areas where you may need to grow or change.

Ultimately, the goal of self-awareness in nonverbal communication is not to become perfect or to eliminate all flaws or quirks, but rather to develop a more authentic, intentional, and flexible communication style that allows you to connect with others in meaningful and impactful ways.

Conscious Control: Learning to Regulate and Refine Your Body Language for Desired Effects

Once you have developed greater self-awareness of your nonverbal patterns and tendencies, the next step in mastering your own communication is learning to consciously regulate and refine your body language, facial expressions, and vocal cues for desired effects. This involves setting clear intentions for how you want to be perceived and what you want to accomplish in a given interaction, and then deliberately using your nonverbal cues to support and reinforce those intentions.

Some key strategies for developing conscious control of your nonverbal communication include:

- o **Practice power posing**: Research has shown that adopting expansive, open postures (known as "power poses") for just a few minutes before an important interaction can increase feelings of confidence, competence, and assertiveness. Try standing tall with your feet apart, your hands on your hips, and your chest open, or sitting with your arms and legs uncrossed and your body taking up space. Notice how these postures feel in your body, and how they may influence your mindset and presence.

- **Use your breath to regulate your state**: Your breath is a powerful tool for regulating your emotional and physiological state, and can have a significant impact on your nonverbal communication. When you're feeling anxious, stressed, or overwhelmed, try taking a few slow, deep breaths into your belly, and exhaling slowly and completely. Notice how this can help you feel more grounded, centered, and in control, and how it may influence your facial expressions, vocal tone, and overall presence.

- **Experiment with different nonverbal styles**: Another way to develop conscious control of your nonverbal communication is to experiment with different styles and approaches in low-stakes situations, such as with friends or in front of a mirror. Try adopting a more expressive or animated style, with larger gestures and more vocal variety, or a more calm and centered style, with stillness and measured movements. Notice how each style feels in your body, and how it may be perceived by others. Look for ways to incorporate elements of different styles into your natural communication repertoire, based on the situation and your desired impact.

- **Focus on your intention and presence**: Finally, the most powerful way to regulate and refine your nonverbal communication is to focus on your underlying intention and presence in the moment. Rather than trying to micromanage every gesture or facial expression, set a clear intention for how you want to show up and what you want to create in the interaction, and then trust your body to communicate that intention authentically. Stay present and attuned to your own experience and the responses of others, and make small adjustments as needed to stay aligned with your goals and values.

Of course, developing conscious control of your nonverbal communication takes time, practice, and a willingness to step outside your comfort zone. It can feel awkward or unnatural at first to deliberately modify your body language or vocal patterns, and you may encounter resistance or setbacks along the way.

Practice and Feedback: Developing Skills Through Observation, Experimentation, and Feedback

Like any skill, mastering your own nonverbal communication requires ongoing practice, experimentation, and feedback. This involves seeking out opportunities to observe and learn from others, trying out new techniques and approaches in real-world situations, and soliciting input and guidance from trusted sources to refine and improve your skills over time.

Some key strategies for practicing and getting feedback on your nonverbal communication include:

- **Observe and model effective communicators**: One of the best ways to improve your own nonverbal skills is to study and learn from others who are highly effective communicators in your field or area of interest. Attend speeches, presentations, or meetings where you can observe how they use their body language, facial expressions, and vocal cues to engage and persuade their audience. Notice what works well and what doesn't, and look for elements you can adapt and incorporate into your own style.

- **Practice in low-stakes situations**: Another valuable way to develop your nonverbal skills is to practice them in low-stakes situations where the consequences of failure are minimal. This might include practicing a presentation in front of a mirror, role-playing a difficult conversation with a friend, or striking up a conversation with a stranger in a coffee shop. Use these opportunities to experiment with different techniques and approaches, and notice how they feel in your body and how they are received by others.
- **Seek out feedback from trusted sources**: To truly refine and improve your nonverbal communication skills, it's essential to seek out feedback from others who can provide an outside perspective and constructive guidance. This might include asking a colleague or mentor to observe you in a meeting or presentation and provide specific feedback on your body language and vocal cues, or seeking out a communication coach or workshop to help you identify areas for growth and development. Be open to hearing both positive and negative feedback, and use it as an opportunity to learn and improve.
- **Embrace a growth mindset**: Finally, the most important factor in developing your nonverbal communication skills is embracing a growth mindset, which sees challenges and setbacks as opportunities for learning and improvement rather than as signs of failure or inadequacy. Recognize that mastering your own nonverbal language is a lifelong journey, and that even the most skilled communicators are always working to refine and adapt their techniques. Celebrate your successes and progress along the way, and use any obstacles or failures as fuel for further growth and development.

Getting feedback on your nonverbal communication can

be uncomfortable or even intimidating at times, especially if you're not used to being in the spotlight or receiving constructive criticism. It's important to approach this process with patience, self-compassion, and a willingness to step outside your comfort zone, knowing that the benefits of improved communication skills will far outweigh any short-term discomfort.

It's about developing a style and presence that feels true to who you are, and that allows you to express yourself fully and authentically in any situation. By staying connected to your own values, goals, and personality, and by using your nonverbal skills as a tool for connection and impact rather than manipulation or control, you can become a more effective and fulfilled communicator in all your personal and professional relationships.

Authenticity vs. Manipulation: Ethical Considerations in Using Nonverbal Communication

As we've seen throughout this book, nonverbal communication is a powerful tool for building rapport, influencing others, and achieving our goals in personal and professional settings. However, with this power comes a great responsibility to use our skills ethically and responsibly, in ways that respect the autonomy and well-being of others and that align with our own values and integrity.

One of the key ethical considerations in using nonverbal communication is the distinction between authenticity and manipulation. Authenticity involves using our nonverbal cues to express our true thoughts, feelings, and intentions in a way that is genuine, transparent, and respectful of others. Manipulation, on the other hand, involves using our nonverbal skills to deceive, control, or exploit others for our own benefit, often at the expense of their needs or well-being.

Some examples of manipulative or unethical uses of nonverbal communication might include:

- Using charm or charisma to seduce someone into a sexual or romantic relationship that is not in their best interest
- Using power poses or intimidating body language to bully or coerce others into complying with our demands
- Using mirroring or mimicry to create a false sense of rapport or trust in order to sell a product or service that is not actually beneficial
- Using strategic eye contact or vocal cues to dominate a conversation or shut down dissenting opinions in a group setting

While these tactics may be effective in the short term for getting what we want, they ultimately erode trust, respect, and connection in our relationships, and can lead to negative consequences for both ourselves and others in the long run.

In contrast, authentic and ethical uses of nonverbal communication involve:

- Using open and welcoming body language to create a sense of safety and inclusion in our interactions
- Using genuine facial expressions and vocal tones to convey our true emotions and intentions, even when they may be difficult or uncomfortable
- Using active listening and empathy to understand and validate others' perspectives and needs, even when they differ from our own
- Using assertive but respectful communication to set boundaries, express our own needs and opinions, and negotiate win-win solutions in conflicts or

disagreements

By approaching our nonverbal communication with authenticity, integrity, and a commitment to mutual understanding and growth, we can build stronger, more meaningful relationships and make a positive impact in the world around us.

Navigating the ethical dimensions of nonverbal communication is not always easy or clear-cut, and there may be times when our intentions and actions do not align perfectly with our values or the needs of others. In these moments, it's important to practice self-reflection, humility, and a willingness to learn from our mistakes and make amends when necessary.

Our nonverbal abilities can be used to create more authentic, fulfilling, and impactful relationships in all areas of our lives through the cultivation of a strong ethical foundation and commitment to personal and interpersonal growth.

Mastering nonverbal communication is not a panacea for all our personal and professional challenges, and that true success and fulfillment require a holistic approach that encompasses our mental, emotional, and spiritual well-being as well as our communication skills. By integrating our nonverbal mastery with a broader commitment to personal growth, self-awareness, and service to others, we can become more effective, authentic, and purposeful communicators and leaders in all our endeavors.

CONCLUSION

The Ongoing Journey of Learning: The Art of Reading People is a Continuous Process of Observation, Analysis, and Adaptation

As we come to the end of this exploration of the art and science of reading people, it's important to recognize that mastering nonverbal communication is not a one-time event or a finite skill set, but rather an ongoing journey of learning, growth, and adaptation. Just as the world around us is constantly changing and evolving, so too are the ways in which we express ourselves and connect with others through our body language, facial expressions, and vocal cues.

To truly excel at reading people and communicating effectively, we must approach this process with a mindset of continuous curiosity, humility, and flexibility. This means being willing to observe and learn from the nonverbal behaviors and interactions we encounter in our daily lives, to analyze and reflect on our own patterns and tendencies, and to adapt our strategies and techniques to the unique needs and contexts of each situation.

Some key principles to keep in mind as we continue our journey of learning and growth in nonverbal communication include:

- **Embrace a beginner's mind**: No matter how much experience or expertise we may have in reading people, there is always more to learn and discover. By approaching each interaction with fresh eyes and an open mind, we can avoid the trap of assumptions or

stereotypes, and remain receptive to new insights and perspectives.
- **Seek out diverse experiences and perspectives**: To truly master the art of reading people, we must expose ourselves to a wide range of individuals, cultures, and contexts, and be willing to learn from the unique nonverbal norms and expectations of each. By seeking out diverse experiences and perspectives, we can expand our understanding of the richness and complexity of human communication, and develop a more inclusive and adaptive approach to our interactions.
- **Practice self-reflection and feedback**: As we've seen throughout this book, developing mastery in nonverbal communication requires ongoing self-awareness, experimentation, and feedback. By taking time to reflect on our own patterns and tendencies, to try out new techniques and approaches, and to seek out constructive input from others, we can continuously refine and improve our skills over time.
- **Cultivate empathy and compassion**: At its core, the art of reading people is about understanding and connecting with others on a deep, authentic level. To truly excel in this process, we must cultivate a strong sense of empathy and compassion, and be willing to put ourselves in others' shoes and see the world through their eyes. By approaching our interactions with kindness, respect, and a genuine desire to understand and support others, we can build more meaningful and impactful relationships in all areas of our lives.

The Importance of Empathy and Respect: Understanding Others Without Judgment or Manipulation

As we've explored throughout this book, the art of reading people is a powerful tool for understanding, connecting with, and influencing others in our personal and professional lives. However, with this power comes a great responsibility to use our skills and insights in ways that are ethical, respectful, and empowering to all involved.

At the heart of this responsibility is the practice of empathy and respect - the ability to put ourselves in others' shoes, to see the world through their eyes, and to honor their unique perspectives, needs, and boundaries. When we approach our interactions with empathy and respect, we create a safe and supportive space for authentic communication, mutual understanding, and positive change.

Some key principles to keep in mind as we cultivate empathy and respect in our nonverbal communication include:

- **Suspend judgment and assumptions**: One of the biggest barriers to empathy and respect is the tendency to judge or make assumptions about others based on their appearance, behavior, or background. By learning to suspend our judgments and assumptions, and to approach each interaction with curiosity and openness, we can create more space for genuine understanding and connection.
- **Listen actively and attentively**: Another key aspect of empathy and respect is the ability to listen deeply and attentively to others, not just with our ears but with our whole being. This means paying attention to their nonverbal cues and emotional states, asking clarifying questions, and reflecting back what we've heard to ensure mutual understanding. By practicing active and empathetic listening, we can build stronger, more trusting relationships and gain valuable insights into others' experiences and perspectives.
- **Honor diversity and difference**: In a world of increasing diversity and complexity, it's essential to cultivate empathy and respect for those who may be different from us in terms of culture, background,

identity, or belief. This means being willing to learn about and appreciate the unique nonverbal norms and expectations of different groups and individuals, and to adapt our own communication style to create more inclusive and equitable interactions. By honoring diversity and difference, we can build bridges of understanding and collaboration across boundaries and divides.

o **Use influence responsibly and ethically**: Finally, as we develop our skills in reading people and influencing others through nonverbal communication, it's crucial to use these skills responsibly and ethically, in ways that respect others' autonomy, dignity, and well-being. This means being transparent about our intentions and motives, seeking consent and agreement before using persuasive techniques, and being willing to accept feedback and adjust our approach when necessary. By using our influence in service of others' growth and empowerment, rather than for personal gain or manipulation, we can create more positive and sustainable change in the world.

There will inevitably be moments when we fall short of our ideals, or when our efforts to understand and connect with others are met with resistance or misunderstanding. In these moments, it's important to practice self-compassion and resilience, and to use our challenges as opportunities for deeper reflection and growth.

Cultivating empathy and respect in the art of reading people is to approach it as a sacred practice - a way of honoring the inherent worth and dignity of all human beings, and of creating more loving, just, and compassionate relationships and communities. By grounding ourselves in these values and principles, and by continually striving to align our nonverbal communication with our highest ideals and aspirations, we can become not just skilled readers of people, but true agents of positive change and transformation in the world.

At the same time, it's important to recognize that empathy and respect are not just individual practices, but collective responsibilities that require the active participation and support of our families, organizations, and societies. By working together to create cultures and systems that prioritize empathy, respect, and inclusion, and by holding ourselves and each other accountable to these values in our daily interactions and decisions, we can build a world where all people are seen, heard, and valued for who they truly are.

Building Stronger Relationships: Using Nonverbal Skills for Better Communication and Deeper Connections

Remember that the ultimate goal of mastering nonverbal communication is not just to be a skilled observer or influencer, but to build stronger, more authentic, and more fulfilling relationships with others. Whether in our personal lives or professional roles, the quality of our connections with others is one of the most important determinants of our happiness, success, and overall well-being.

By developing our skills in reading and responding to nonverbal cues, we can create more effective, empathetic, and engaging interactions with others, and foster deeper levels of trust, understanding, and collaboration. Some key ways that nonverbal communication can help us build stronger relationships include:

- **Enhancing emotional intelligence and empathy**: By learning to read and interpret others' facial expressions, body language, and vocal tones, we can gain valuable insights into their emotional states, needs, and perspectives, and respond in ways that show understanding, care, and support. This kind of emotional intelligence and empathy is essential for building strong, trusting relationships, both personally and professionally.

- **Improving communication and conflict resolution**: Nonverbal communication plays a crucial role in how we express ourselves and navigate difficult conversations or conflicts with others. By using open, non-threatening body language, maintaining appropriate eye contact, and modulating our tone of voice, we can create a more positive and constructive atmosphere for communication, and work towards mutually satisfying solutions and agreements.
- **Increasing influence and leadership**: As we've seen throughout this book, nonverbal communication is a powerful tool for influencing and motivating others, whether in sales, management, or other leadership roles. By projecting confidence, warmth, and authenticity through our body language and vocal cues, we can inspire trust, respect, and loyalty in others, and create more effective and cohesive teams and organizations.
- **Deepening intimacy and connection**: Finally, nonverbal communication is essential for building and maintaining close, intimate relationships with romantic partners, family members, and friends. By attuning to each other's nonverbal cues and rhythms, expressing affection and care through touch and gesture, and creating shared moments of laughter, play, and vulnerability, we can foster deeper levels of emotional and physical intimacy, and create more fulfilling and lasting bonds with those we love.

So as you go forth from this book, I encourage you to embrace the ongoing journey of learning and growth that lies ahead, and to use your newfound knowledge and skills to make a positive difference in the lives of those around you. Whether through small acts of kindness and connection in your daily interactions, or through larger efforts to promote justice, equity, and wellbeing in your spheres of influence, you have the power to be a force for good in the world, and to create ripples of positive change that extend far beyond your own life and relationships.

Thank you for joining me on this exploration of the art and science of reading people. I am grateful for your curiosity, your engagement, and your commitment to personal and interpersonal growth, and I look forward to continuing to learn and grow alongside you in the years to come. May your journey be filled with joy, connection, and meaning, and may you always remember the incredible power and potential that lies within you to create a better world, one interaction at a time.

This content is provided for informational and educational purposes only and should not be construed as professional advice or a substitute for seeking appropriate professional assistance. The information presented herein is based on the authors' personal experiences, research, and opinions, which may not be suitable or applicable for all individuals or situations.

The authors, publishers, and distributors have made reasonable efforts to ensure the accuracy and timeliness of the information contained herein. However, they do not guarantee the completeness, suitability, or applicability of this information for any specific individual, situation, or purpose. The authors, publishers, and distributors shall not be held liable for any direct, indirect, incidental, or consequential damages resulting from the use or misuse of the information provided.

It is strongly recommended that readers seek professional advice and guidance from qualified professionals in their respective fields, such as financial advisors, legal counsel, medical practitioners, or certified coaches, for their specific situations and needs.

No part of this content may be reproduced, distributed, or transmitted in any form or by any means, including photocopying, recording, or other electronic or mechanical methods, without the prior written permission of the authors or copyright holders.

For other books and resources that may interest you, please click here:

SARAH THOMPSON

https://know.howtoalways.win/sarahthompson

www.ingramcontent.com/pod-product-compliance
Lightning Source LLC
Chambersburg PA
CBHW071210240526
45470CB00018B/1693